SUCCESS
Behind the Scars

ALDRIC MARSHALL

SUCCESS
Behind the Scars

IT'S NOT WHAT YOU HAVE THAT MAKES YOU SUCCESSFUL.
IT'S WHAT YOU'VE DONE WITH THE SCARS THAT DEFINES YOUR SUCCESS.

Tate Publishing & *Enterprises*

Success Behind the Scars
Copyright © 2008 by Aldric Marshall. All rights reserved.

This title is also available as a Tate Out Loud product. Visit www.tatepublishing.com for more information.

No part of this publication may be reproduced, stored in a retrieval system or transmitted in any way by any means, electronic, mechanical, photocopy, recording or otherwise without the prior permission of the author except as provided by USA copyright law.

Scripture quotations marked "NIV" are taken from the *Holy Bible, New International Version* ®, Copyright © 1973, 1978, 1984 by International Bible Society. Used by permission of Zondervan Publishing House. All rights reserved.

This book is designed to provide accurate and authoritative information with regard to the subject matter covered. This information is given with the understanding that neither the author nor Tate Publishing, LLC is engaged in rendering legal, professional advice. Since the details of your situation are fact dependent, you should additionally seek the services of a competent professional.

The opinions expressed by the author are not necessarily those of Tate Publishing, LLC.

Published by Tate Publishing & Enterprises, LLC
127 E. Trade Center Terrace | Mustang, Oklahoma 73064 USA
1.888.361.9473 | www.tatepublishing.com

Tate Publishing is committed to excellence in the publishing industry. The company reflects the philosophy established by the founders, based on Psalm 68:11,
"The Lord gave the word and great was the company of those who published it."

Book design copyright © 2008 by Tate Publishing, LLC. All rights reserved.
Cover design by Kellie Southerland
Interior design by Melanie Harr-Hughes

Published in the United States of America

ISBN: 978-1-60696-358-6
1. Autobiographical   2. Religious
08.10.07

Dedication

This book is dedicated first to my Lord and Savior Jesus Christ, for without the trials there would be no testimony. Secondly, to my wife Kim, whose constant support and loving encouragement provided the spark necessary to make this dream a reality. And last to my children, Kaleb and Keturah. Thank you for believing in your dad.

Acknowledgement

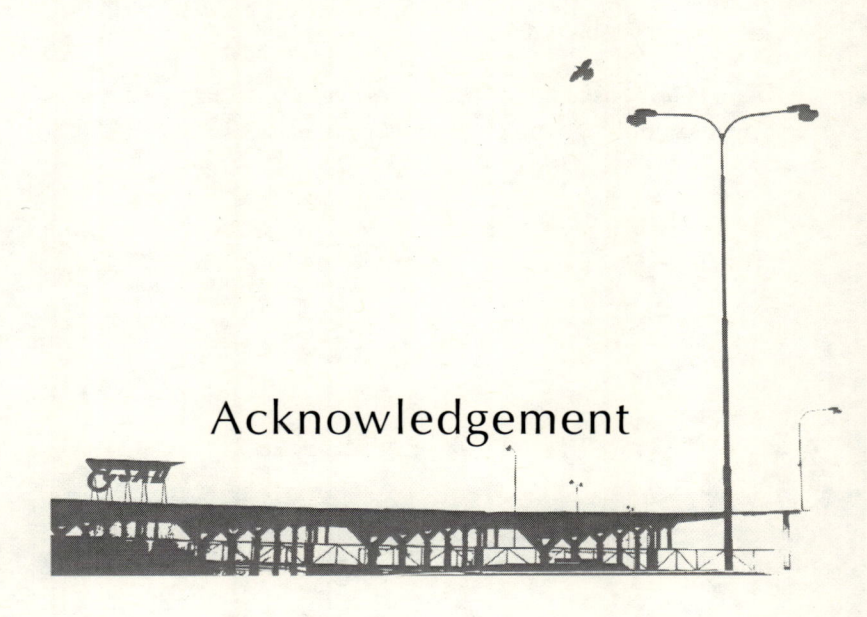

The acknowledgement of a book most people care not to read. For the author, however, it is a priceless opportunity to express appreciation to some important people.

My deepest gratitude is extended to Bernice and Willie Ferguson who constantly pray for my family and prayed relentlessly for this project.

Thank you Don Powell, Bryan Boysaw, Bryan Williams, and Jimmy Bell for your excitement about the book and for staying on me to complete it.

To my entire family, thank you for your encouragement, patience, and belief in my ability to produce my first book.

Listing all of the family, friends, co-workers, and professional acquaintances who continually influence my life is not possible. Suffice it to say the truth in this book would not be possible without them.

Table of Contents

Chapter 1 | Success Is A Choice | 15

Chapter 2 | Those Rough Early Years | 27

Chapter 3 | Fear of Being Exposed | 47

Chapter 4 | My Brief Air Force Stint | 67

Chapter 5 | "You'll Never Leave the Scrap Yard!" | 83

Chapter 6 | Layoffs and Mean Dogs | 99

Chapter 7 | Barber School Break | 113

Chapter 8 | Finding My Way | 125

Chapter 9 | Playing Spiritual Catch-up | 139

Chapter 10 | Getting Others Motivated | 153

Chapter 11 | Cured from M.S. | 173

Chapter 12 | Building Healthy Lives, Healthy Communities | 197

Chapter 13 | The Keys to Overcome Your Scars | 209

Foreword

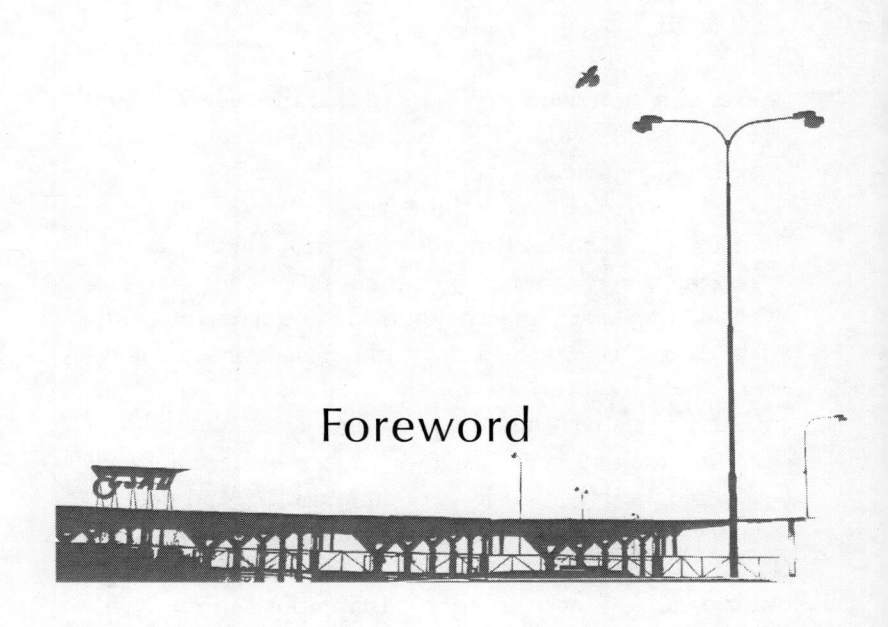

When my co-author and I were conducting research for our book, *Dream It Do It: Inspiring Stories of Dreams Come True*, we spoke with dozens of people who overcame obstacles to reach their dreams. What we discovered is that every dream achiever masters at least one of the following personal attributes: courage, confidence, creativity, commitment, persistence, passion, purpose, risk, resilience, or responsibility. We dubbed these attributes the "Ten Elements of Dream CPR" because they work to resuscitate a person's dreams just as the emergency medical procedure CPR can bring a person back to life.

Everybody has these ten elements to some degree, although they may remain hidden, inactive, or even dormant for most of one's life. The trick is to bring these qualities out and actively develop them over time, with every life experience. We noticed that the more a person exercises these ten attributes, the more likely he or she will achieve a heartfelt dream.

I have to tell you, Aldric Marshall possesses *all* ten of these Dream CPR qualities in great abundance. He has the courage to overcome the scars he's acquired as a child, a teenager, and an adult. He possesses the confidence to pursue his dreams without reservation, knowing that God provides what he needs to reach his goals. Aldric's creativity has, time and time again, allowed him to find exciting new avenues whenever he's encountered roadblocks. His high level of commitment and dedication enable him to see a goal to fruition.

Aldric has the persistence to keep working towards his dreams, a sense of purpose that propels him to work on something bigger than himself and the passion to give every venture more than a hundred percent. He is not afraid to take risks. When he encounters setbacks or experiences failure, he has the resilience to get back up and keep moving forward. And he has a highly developed sense of responsibility that enables him to dream not only for himself but also for his family, his community, and humanity as a whole. Aldric always strives to help as many people as possible as he works towards building strong, healthy communities. He is a dreamer and a doer of the highest caliber.

In the following pages, you'll read his true story. You'll see how he overcame challenges of his youth and setbacks of his adult years to create a richly rewarding, meaningful, and successful life for himself. Even when things looked grim, Aldric never, ever lost hope. He continues to actively seek, find, and create solutions to bring him up to the next level. Most inspiring of all, he brings people up with him at every step. He's one of those remarkable individuals who openly shares what he's learned, without reservation, so that others can benefit from his experiences.

In Aldric's story you'll find humor, angst, hope, and inspiration. You'll also see yourself in certain passages. Some of what Aldric went through is universal, while some is unique to his life story. Through the ups and downs and the lessons he learned, he shares insights to help you along your own journey. Aldric offers sage advice combined with doses of inspiration to propel you to achieve your special dreams. He achieved, and so can you. Let his true story inspire you to take the first, second, and following steps to the life that *you* were meant to live!

Graciela Sholander,
International Author

CHAPTER 1
Success Is A Choice

Most successful men have not achieved their distinction by having some new talent or opportunity presented to them.

They have developed the opportunity that was at hand.

Bruce Barton,
author, advertiser, politician

Success Is A Choice

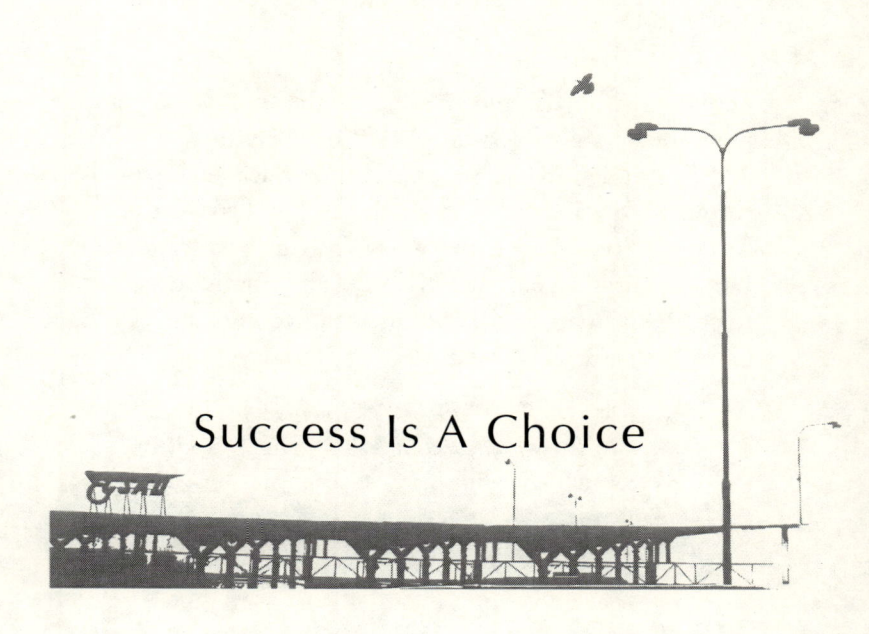

I wasn't supposed to succeed. Plenty of people along the way told me I wouldn't amount to anything. They said I'd be stuck in low-wage jobs. That I'd grow up to be a wife-beater. That I'd drift from one dead-end job to another, never making much money, never contributing to society.

I'm happy to report that they were wrong.

My fulfilling marriage to my high school sweetheart is sixteen years strong, and we have the utmost respect for each other. I'm a loving, responsible dad to my children. I've enjoyed many rewarding jobs including facility operator for a multi-million dollar operation, hair salon entrepreneur, realtor, high school police aide, safe school ambassador facilitator, and motivational speaker.

I'm the founder of "Connecting The World With The Word Ministries," a program that trains church parishioners to do ministry out in the "real world" and win others to Christ. I completed college with a 3.8 GPA, and I've honed my public speaking and leadership skills through Toastmasters International and Dale Carnegie Training. Together with my wife Kim, I've launched Urban Youth Development (UYD), an initiative designed to create business leaders out of urban young men. And I haven't even reached my fortieth birthday yet.

> None of us will ever accomplish anything excellent or commanding except when he listens to this whisper which is heard by him alone.
>
> *Ralph Waldo Emerson*

For someone with my background, it's not supposed to turn out this way. Those doomsayers saw the environment I was raised in, heard the labels I'd been given, and decided I'd be a failure in life. I grew up amidst violent fighting in my home with my brother, sister, and me constantly trying to protect our mother from our father's fists. At school I defended my siblings and myself against tough kids who got a kick out of bullying us. During my earliest formative years, we lived in a poor neighborhood swarming with drug dealers.

What's more, I couldn't read. I was labeled a slow learner, and I barely graduated from high school with a 2.0 GPA. I was kicked out of the Air Force for failing a qualifying test and had to get a job in a hot, dirty scrap yard where I salvaged metal from dismantled airplane engines. Talk about boring and tedious.

When I relate my past to people, they find it hard to

comprehend. Invariably they ask, "Aldric, how did you overcome your past struggles to be successful?" Good question. How does a kid who can't read grow up to earn top grades in a challenging university program? How does a child who witnesses his father beating up his mother later become a loving husband?

> The art of life is to know how to enjoy a little and to endure much.
>
> *William Hazlitt*

The answers to these and other success-related questions are what *Success Behind The Scars* endeavors to illuminate. Within these pages you'll find the story of my life, but more than that you'll get a straightforward look at what it takes to rise above the clouds of fear just enough to see that the sun's been shining all along. No doubt about it, life has its frightening moments. We all collect scars along our journey. I've certainly accumulated my share. But I refused to let the wounds and fears stop me from moving forward with my dreams. Don't let your fears kill *your* dreams, my friend. Instead of allowing yourself to get dragged down by fear, choose to rise above and strive for something better. By doing this you align yourself in the direction of success.

Every one of us has major hurdles to overcome. Sadly, not everyone has figured out how to overcome theirs. Some folks decide that it's too hard to get ahead, and they choose to give up. They decide that it's more comfortable to stay right where they are, even if they're miserable, just because the known is a lot less frightening than the unknown. Do you realize that many people are more afraid of success than they are of failure? Truthfully, you shouldn't be afraid of either, because every success is always preceded by a series of failures.

When you fail at something, it's *not* the end of the world. Congratulate yourself for trying! Maybe it didn't turn out the way you'd hoped, but all is not lost. You may not realize it yet, but you've gained so much. For starters, you've acquired knowledge and experience that will help you in your next attempt. When you try enough times, you ultimately succeed.

> Failure after long perseverance is much grander than never to have a striving good enough to be called a failure.
>
> *George Eliot*

It takes courage to keep trying. You need resilience to bounce back and keep going. Believe me, God has given you these qualities. You were born with a measure of courage and resilience, and through life's trials you have the chance to grow further in these important traits. If you choose to seize the opportunity, that is.

When I got kicked out of the Air Force, it was one of the saddest days of my life. I loved being in the Air Force. I fit in. I moved up quickly and was selected to serve as platoon leader. My sergeant hated to see me go, but rules are rules and failing the test meant I couldn't stay.

I could have gotten myself into a funk after that. I could have blamed others, blamed the system, or blamed society for my troubles, but I didn't. As sad as I was to end that brief military chapter of my life, I saw it as an opportunity. I still had my dreams burning in my heart. Instead of giving up, I vowed to do whatever it took to succeed in my next venture.

When you see every experience as a step in your personal self-development, you empower yourself to keep going, keep trying, and keep moving forward. A failed attempt is nothing more than a learning experience. Accumulate enough of them, and you're bound to succeed.

If I had to boil down the secret to success into its simplest form, it would be this: *persistence and hope.* You don't just throw your hands up in the air and give up when life gets rough. You keep trying again, and again, and again. Try as many times as you need to, as long as it takes until you get to where you want to be. Anyone who's enjoyed success has had to become good friends with persistence.

Hope is just as important, because hope keeps you positive in the face of pain, troubles, suffering, and adversity. Hope is a picture you hold in your mind of a better life for yourself. It's the feeling in your heart that propels you forward even when the chips are down. A good definition for the word "hope" is: *To wish for something with expectation of its fulfillment.* You're not just wishing upon a star you fully expect what you wish for to come to pass, and you act accordingly. By taking action, you take steps to reach your goal.

> For us is the life of action, of strenuous performance of duty; let us live in the harness, striving mightily; let us rather run the risk of wearing out than rusting out.
>
> *Theodore Roosevelt*

The hope and persistence success formula wouldn't be complete without God in the picture. Every step of the way I've felt God guiding me. Sometimes His presence is subtle, and other times He's there in a huge way, but always God is there. I'm sure that if you stop to think about it, you'll see that God's been playing a key role in your life, too. Those little coincidences, the times when things just fell into place almost as if by magic, and the second chances. Who do you think is behind all that?

Rounding out the success equation is community. For every person who doubted or dismissed me, there was someone who cared, someone to lift me up. Be it a family member, a school official, a neighborhood mentor, or a friend, there's always been somebody in my life to share a laugh with, to serve as a role model, or to show me that by applying myself, I *can* do it. Community is a vital, life-enhancing, two-way street. There comes a time when it's your turn to reach out a helping hand, say that encouraging word, and stand up and do the right thing for your fellow human.

Hope. Persistence. God. Community. This is how a person prevails over the scars of his or her life to define success. This is how you can start to turn your life around and ultimately achieve your own success. It doesn't matter who you are or where you've been. It doesn't matter how disadvantaged or unprepared you feel you *have* the wherewithal to overcome your struggles, to reach your dreams, or to help others along the way. This is the true measure of success. It's not about what you have or don't have. It's what you've chosen to do to rise above that makes the difference.

Success Story

Paul Robeson, Actor, Athlete, Singer, Writer, Speaker & Activist

Paul LeRoy Bustill Robeson was a man of many firsts, breaking barriers to succeed in numerous pursuits. Born in New Jersey in 1898, Paul became an accomplished actor, athlete, concert singer, writer, and right's activist. He had an amazing talent with the spoken and written word, attaining fluency in twelve languages and becoming conversant in twenty!

These are just some of his many achievements:

- Graduated from high school with honors
- Graduated from Rutgers University as class valedictorian
- Was a professional football player
- Earned a law degree
- Became a stage actor, winning acclaim and honors for his performances
- Became a concert singer
- Sang in several languages, including Chinese, German, and Yiddish
- Toured the world through his performances
- Appeared in eleven movies

- Became an activist for African Americans and Asian Americans
- Co-founded the Council on African Affairs
- Spoke in many countries championing rights and freedom for all people
- Received an award for outstanding achievement by the NAACP

Along with the phenomenal success, though, he acquired many scars. He was physically assaulted by fellow football players who didn't want him on the team. When he was an attorney, a secretary refused to take dictation from him because of the color of his skin. Paul experienced racism and discrimination at every turn, barred from restaurants and other establishments. He enjoyed starring roles in Shakespeare productions in England but not in his native United States until many years later. Because of his sympathies towards the Soviet Union, where he felt that black people received equal treatment, unlike in the U.S. at the time, he was wrongly labeled a communist. His political views incited riots. In 1950 his passport was denied, preventing him from leaving the United States; it was not returned to him until eight years later.

Despite the many scars, Paul did everything in his power to reach his dreams. He continued to tour the world, sharing his singing and acting talents with appreciative audiences. He continued to speak for the oppressed, including Welsh miners and Basque refugees. For his efforts and achievements, Paul received countless honors and awards from groups around the globe. He had the courage to live his dreams and speak his mind, even when his views were unpopular. In the process of pursuing his dreams, he created an amazing life for himself.

CHAPTER 2
Those Rough Early Years

The question is not whether we can afford to invest in every child; it is whether we can afford not to.

Marian Wright Edelman,
children's right's activist

Those Rough Early Years

In the cool shade of my aunt's gigantic fruit tree, our superhero dramas played out. My big brother, Alpheaus, was Batman the Brave. Our cousin was trusty sidekick Robin. And once again I was stuck playing the villain, this time the Joker or "The Clown Prince Of Crime." They never let me be the superhero. I was perpetually the bad guy, the one getting chased, captured, tied up, handcuffed, and pushed around.

We had free rein of my aunt's backyard, with one exception: *Do not climb the tree.* The rule was in place for a good reason. My aunt didn't want any of us kids falling down and getting seriously hurt. It was an immense tree, reaching way up to the sky just like in the old fairy tale, *Jack and the Beanstalk*. Scaling that tree was strictly forbidden.

On that particular sunny afternoon, rules beckoned

to be broken. No more "Mr. Bad Guy." I was done being mistreated. Sulking, I started climbing up that old tree. Up and up I went, each step putting more distance between me and the boys. Without looking down, I kept climbing higher and higher... until I got stuck. Wedged between two large branches, I could not get myself out. "Alpheaus, I'm stuck!"

> Men grow to the stature to which they are stretched when they are young.
>
> *Antony Jay*

He shook his head and then nimbly climbed to the spot where I was. He tugged at me and pulled on the branches, but I didn't budge. He scurried back to the ground, and my cousin came up to give it a try, but I was really stuck. He went back down to strategize with Alpheaus. I could hear them talking about getting my aunt but only as a last resort. When she gave you a beating for disobeying, she didn't mess around. They took turns climbing up again and again, trying to free me from the tree's firm grasp.

By their fourth unsuccessful attempt, I was scared and crying. In defeat and exhaustion, my brother and cousin ran to the house to get my aunt. From my bird's-eye view through the branches, I saw the sliding glass door glide open. Out stepped my aunt, a matronly woman in her fifties, cigarette dangling from her mouth. With her left hand on her hip, she squinted towards the bright blue sky and spotted me. Pausing for just a moment, she tossed her cigarette down to the patio floor and stomped it out.

My aunt bolted across the patio, across the grass, and started up the tree like a thirteen-year-old girl climbing with precision. She reached me and, hanging on with one arm, used her other arm to tug at the branches that held me prisoner. She did it. I was free! I scrambled down to safety with my aunt right behind me.

> No passion so effectually robs the mind of all its powers of acting and reasoning as fear.
>
> *Edmund Burke*

Amazingly, I was spared a whooping. Maybe because I was so young, or maybe because my clown nature took over, and I was able to joke my way out of punishment. The other two weren't so lucky. They got the belt. I hadn't planned it, but I guess in a way, I got my revenge on them for always making me be the bad guy.

Brothers & Sis

In truth, I adored my brother. I looked up to him as my role model. Three years older than me, Alpheaus inherited the gift of music from my mother's side of the family and had a fabulous singing voice. I tried singing, but I wasn't any good. Then I tried playing the drums, but all I managed to do was make a lot of noise. I tried the guitar, too. My big brother played it like you wouldn't believe, so, of course, I wanted to play the guitar. I learned how to strum a little, but I could never make the guitar sing the way he did.

My brother was like a father to me, but he hadn't volunteered for that role. He was a loner who didn't talk a whole lot. He didn't have to. From a distance I watched what he did and tried to be just like him. Even though I was the youngest in my family and a really small kid physically—I came up to everybody's midsection—I always defended my brother with my fists at school. I wouldn't let anyone mistreat him.

> A family divided against itself will perish together
> *Anonymous*

Alpheus' quiet nature didn't stop him from joining forces with me to play pranks on our sister, Erica. She's two years older than me, and I love her to death. My brother and I made sure nobody else put a hand on our sister, but we sure liked to pick on her.

Our dog, Tiger, was great around guys but not so good with girls. We'd trick Erica into going outside with us, and then we'd take off running and leave her alone with the dog. Tiger never bit her, thank goodness, but he definitely intimidated Erica with all that growling and snarling.

Every year the circus came around, preceded by a festive parade. The whole town turned up to watch the elephants, giraffes, and tigers being loaded off the train and paraded before us en route to the big auditorium in the middle of town, where the show was held. My brother, sister, and I loved going to the circus.

I was playing outside my grandmother's house with

Alpheus while the circus was setting up; Erica was inside keeping Grandma company. I was seven years old. My brother and I came across a deep hole. It fascinated us. We estimated it to be seven or eight, maybe even nine feet. As we peered into the depths, we looked up at each other and smiled. We both had the exact same idea.

We found a large piece of corrugated cardboard and used it to cover the hole. Then we called Erica outside and quite nonchalantly led her to the concealed hole. It worked like a charm. In she fell. We laughed hysterically. Somehow, she managed to climb out, but one of her shoes stayed behind, lost in the cavernous depths. Our laughter stopped abruptly when our grandmother came out. Yeah, we got in trouble, and we didn't get to go to the circus.

My sister always amazed me. She never, not once, tried pulling tricks back on us. She was a lot more mature than we ever were. It simply wasn't in her nature to be mean, or envious, or jealous for that matter. On the contrary, she was our protector. When my father beat me with a belt, Erica boldly stepped in. She looked straight at our dad with her head held high and firmly said, "You're not going to put a hand on him no more." Then she looked at me and, like a little mommy, tenderly said, "It's okay. You're alright now. Don't worry." My father stopped hitting me. I could see him smiling in amusement and maybe even a touch of pride.

Young Protectors

Sure, my brother and sister and I fussed and fought among ourselves, but we were close. We had to be, because we had a very serious responsibility at such a young age. We were our mother's protectors. My mom and dad fought all the time. I felt I'd been robbed of the opportunity to grow up in a peaceful home during my young, formative years. Time and again, when Dad started beating Mom up, we three would rush in and start pounding on him until he stopped.

We lived just north of West Palm Beach in Riviera Beach, Florida, where I was born. Our home was on 32nd Street and S Avenue, where poverty prevailed and drug dealers and users flourished. Dad was a construction worker who did concrete work for both the commercial and residential sectors. Mom had a large clientele as a popular and well-liked cosmetologist. She was self-employed, renting a chair at the local beauty salon. Mom left for work bright and early every morning, including Saturdays. While she worked, our next-door neighbor, Momma Panky, watched over us kids.

> Above all we need, particularly as children, the reassuring presence of a visible community, an intimate group that enfolds us with understanding and love, and that becomes an object of our spontaneous loyalty, as a criterion and point of reference for the rest of the human race.
>
> *Lewis Mumford*

Just about every African-American family in my town back then had a "Big Momma" who helped with the kids. I spent most of my early childhood days with Momma Panky, a really nice, caring, elderly woman, our very own Big Momma. Over the years, I'm sure I walked thousands of times back and forth through the side gate that separated our houses. Momma Panky was my second mother, but she took care of me like I was her own. So in a sense, I had two homes. Most days, I preferred the safe haven of Momma Panky's to the chaos in my own home.

The majority of my early childhood memories are plagued by images of my mother and biological father arguing and physically fighting each other. Mom tried to protect us, to conceal the fighting from us, but there was no hiding it. We came home from church one afternoon, and my parents got into another one of their knock-out fights in their bedroom. Mom closed the door to shield us from the violence. We still heard the loud screaming and yelling, though.

> All violence...is not power but the absence of power.
>
> *Ralph Waldo Emerson*

Like miniature World Wrestling Federation fighters, the three of us busted through that door and went to work on our dad. We found him on top of our mom, punching her. Alpheaus jumped up on the bed and brought his elbow down on Dad's back with such force that he was temporarily immobilized and stopped hitting Mom. Meanwhile, Erica ran off to the kitchen to boil water in case we needed to throw hot liquid on our father, and I ran to get our bat, a Louisville slugger. Thankfully, we didn't need to use the boiling water or the bat. But that day is forever etched in my mind. That's the day I vowed never to put my future wife and family through such torment. I've kept that promise.

The police came and filed a report. After they left, I followed my dad to my parents' bedroom. He began to pack his bags. Despite everything, I still loved him, and seeing him pack scared me. Just seven years old, I didn't want our family to break up. I didn't want us to become a "divorce statistic." I asked him what he was doing.

"Your mother told me I have to leave," he replied. "She said that at this rate, either I'll end up killing her, or the four of you will end up killing me."

He left that evening and moved in with my grandmother. He continues to live with his mother to this day. That night, I became fatherless. It was for the best, but it still hurt.

> The lust for power is not rooted in strength but in weakness.
>
> *Erich Fromm*

There are no excuses for how he treated Mom, but I always sought to understand why. The closest I got was that Dad had low self-esteem and a big jealousy problem. I believe he felt self-conscious being much older than my mother and having no more than a third-grade education. She was a beautiful, independent woman who had two exciting careers going for her-cosmetology and gospel singing. He was probably afraid she'd walk out on him, and as warped as it sounds, perhaps he reasoned that by creating enough fear in her, she'd never leave him. The day he left, we finally had peace and quiet in our home.

I Learned My Lesson

My mother has a voice like an angel from heaven. She sang with our church and traveled with the choir to sing unto the Lord. I was blessed to have a strong black mother who loved the Lord Jesus and did everything she could to give us a normal life. She was our provider and our protector. She tried to keep us on the straight and narrow path.

My childhood best friend Rodney Ship (we're friends to this day) and I grew up in the same neighborhood. Rodney had a bike that Mom told me not to ride. Our street was busy, and she didn't want me getting hurt. But just like I didn't listen to my aunt and climbed up that giant fruit tree, I didn't listen to Mom and rode my friend's bike. Momma Panky had given me fifty cents, and it was burning a hole in my pocket. Rodney gave me permission to ride his bike to the nearby convenience store.

I stared at the tempting sugary choices for a long time before I made my selection, walked to the counter, and stretched way up to put both the candy and my money on that impossibly tall counter. From the corner of my eye, I saw a much bigger boy jump on Rodney's bike and take off. I ran outside, but the boy was gone. I ran back in. The money and my candy had disappeared, too. I slowly walked back to Rodney's, empty handed and downhearted.

"I'm sorry, but someone stole your bike," I offered. Rodney's mother called my mom at the beauty salon and told her what had happened. She put me on the phone.

"I'm gonna whoop you when I get home!" Mom fired

off. "I told you not to ride that bike. Didn't I tell you? I told you!"

> The mistakes we aren't allowed to make in our youth, we make later on in life at greater cost and with less benefit.
>
> *Anonymous*

I shuffled home and climbed into bed, hoping she'd just forget about the whole ugly mess when she got home from work. Pretty soon, I was fast asleep.

Mom woke me up from a sound sleep. "Go take your bath now. You forgot to do that when you came home." Through the haze of sleep it all started to come back: the bike, the convenience store... oh no, the whooping!

Still groggy, I went to the bathroom and started the water running. I took my clothes off and stepped into the tub. Ouch! Mom popped me right in the bottom with a wet towel. She did it again, and again. I protested and grabbed the towel, trying to keep a firm grasp without falling.

"Let go!" she said.

"No, Mom, I can't do that."

"Let go, Aldric!"

"No!"

"I told you not to get on anybody's bike! See what happened? I told you!"

She was done. The whooping was over. I sat down in the tub and took my bath. Then I got dressed, climbed into bed, and cried myself to sleep. In the morning, Mom came into my room, not a trace of anger left in her. Calmly she explained to me why she did what she had done and why it was important that I listen to her. She always took the time to explain things. Thank goodness she did a lot more talking than punishing.

That Strange Place Called School

I never went to any type of preschool or daycare. Momma Panky was my daycare. She watched over me and hugged me and fed me, and she let me sleep all day long if I wanted to. I had no early learning or socialization opportunities. No phonics, no ABCs, no math, nothing. So that first day of school when Mom drove me to Washington Elementary, fear grabbed a hold of me as soon as I stepped out of the car. I cried my eyes out. I didn't want Mom to leave me there. I wanted to go back to the safe haven of Momma Panky.

In class, I couldn't concentrate. Who were all these people? I didn't know any of them, nor did I care about them. I wanted to go home. I didn't hear a word the teacher said. My mind was consumed by one thought: *While I'm here, Mom and Dad are back home fighting.* I didn't belong in this strange place. I needed to be home to protect Mom. I couldn't wait to be released from this new prison.

A week later, the situation had improved. I'd fallen in love with my first grade teacher, Ms. Jerry. She was young and pretty and the first white person I'd ever met. I was invited to have dinner with her family at her house. To my surprise, Mom allowed me to go. I learned at Ms. Jerry's home that families actually eat together. I was amazed when we sat down around the table and shared a meal together. This never happened at my house. Momma Panky fed my brother, sister, and me, while Mom and Dad grabbed something to eat when they came home from work. We never sat down together at the table as a family.

> Never take counsel from your fears.

Little by little, I accepted school as my new reality, but I remained distracted. When I tried to concentrate on schoolwork, images of Mom and Dad fighting invaded my mind. This continued through first and second grades. They were supposed to be my learning and development years, but I learned very little.

By second grade, I was beating up anyone who tormented my big brother. Because Mom always dressed us well, jealous kids liked to pick on us, especially on Alpheaus. They made fun of everything from our crisp, starched shirts to our neat slacks to our polished shoes. My brother never fought back, so I fought for both of us.

During my third year of elementary school, something fabulous was happening for our family. Mom met a wonderful man, Curtis Donaway. Just like her, he loved the Lord and sang sweet gospel music. They started dating and soon fell head over heels in love. I felt proud to be a part of their small wedding ceremony at the Martin County Courthouse. At first I thought of Curtis as my step-dad, but in time he became Dad. My deep longing for a father figure finally was fulfilled.

Dad brought value to my life. He was a real man who

spent time with me and treated Mom right. I was shocked and amazed that he didn't know how to curse. And I was ecstatic that he didn't like to spank or whip either.

We moved away from our crime-riddled neighborhood to a nice, big house in West Palm Beach that I got to see built from the ground up. A new house with three bedrooms and *two* full baths. More importantly, a brand new start on life. Finally we had the peaceful haven at home I'd wanted my whole young life.

> Peace is a daily, a weekly, a monthly process, gradually changing opinions, slowly eroding old barriers, quietly building new structures.
>
> *John F. Kennedy*

While the situation improved vastly at home, I still struggled at school. The damage had already been done. After missing out on the basics of reading, writing, and math, I had developed a mental block. It was difficult to impossible for me to learn the way other kids learned. I couldn't read, so I didn't learn from books. Instead, I learned by watching others and by hearing and retelling stories. I learned to get by.

I attended fourth grade at Lincoln Elementary, and I adored my teacher, Mrs. King. She had a way with children. I still struggled academically, but at the same time I began to feel a sense of purpose, particularly with my new group of friends. We had a center on the school campus for American Retarded Citizens (ARC). I volunteered to help the individuals there with their daily tasks, everything from wiping their faces to talking with them to helping them go outside during a fire drill. I considered everyone at the center a friend. One friend in particular was Adam, a blind and very cool white kid. Every day I walked him to each of his classes, making sure he arrived on time, before I ran over to mine. It felt good to help. I felt needed. It also made me feel that I was good at something, because in class I worked very hard to hide from everyone, even Mrs. King, my inability to read and learn.

Because I couldn't learn from books, I learned directly from people. From Mr. Holt, my Irish soccer coach with his thick accent and the patience of Job, I learned how to focus my mind on what I was going to do and keep myself disciplined to get it done. Thanks to his expert guidance, our soccer team went undefeated.

> We are here to help each other get through this thing, whatever it is.
>
> *Anonymous*

Then there was Mr. Walker, my first African-American male teacher who really showed me what it means to be a strong black male in society. He was my math teacher, and he knew how to engage us kids. He planted this important seed in me: With time, persistence, and hope you can achieve everything you want to. Just last week, I ran into him at the grocery store as he helped his elderly mother do her shopping. I said to him, "Mr. Walker, I just want to tell you that you impacted my life at Lincoln Elementary many years ago, and I thank you."

He replied, "That's what I'm here for." As I turned away to continue my shopping, I overheard him tell his mother, "That was a kid I taught thirty years ago." No doubt about it, he was a dedicated teacher who truly cared about his students' well being.

I'm thankful to Mr. Fred Alan for keeping me off the streets by teaching me baseball. He was a neighbor of ours who coached at the local recreation center. We started with five on the team, including Mr. Alan's son, and pretty soon all the neighborhood kids were joining in. By watching him and seeing his unselfish nature at work, I learned the importance of putting others first. I also learned to be a darn good pitcher.

And finally, there was my uncle Claude Vereen, my mother's brother. Uncle Claude taught me how to work with my hands and how to capitalize on my strengths. He saw that something wasn't clicking for me in school, so he took it upon himself to show me how to do woodworking, fix cars, change tires, do plumbing, and all sorts of things. Through Uncle Claude, I learned to take pride in using my hands to create and repair.

Even though school was a challenge for me and my biological father was not able to be the role model I needed, I was fortunate to have other role models and mentors in my community. I'm thankful to these men, because they planted seeds that have grown with me and helped me become the man I am today. I learned a great deal from these gentlemen. Their positive effect on me countered the negativity I, unfortunately, heard from some of my relatives, everything from, "Boy, you don't know nothing," to "You are going to be just like your dad."

> Words so innocent and powerless as they are, as standing in a dictionary, how potent for good and evil they become, in the hands of one who knows how to combine them.
>
> *Nathaniel Hawthorne*

In addition to my positive mentors, humor helped me get by. I learned early in life that if I made people laugh, they couldn't stay angry with me for very long. When I was ten, I had a tremendous fascination for my stepfather's razor. He and Mom were off at work, and that razor sitting on the bathroom counter was just too tempting for me. I decided I was old enough to try my hand at shaving. So I lathered shaving cream on my face and very carefully picked up Dad's razor. I looked in the mirror, and that's when I realized that I had no hair to shave. Except for my eyebrows.

A quick swish-swish, and my right eyebrow was gone. What had I done? I couldn't believe how strange I looked with that eyebrow missing. Mom and Dad would surely notice the moment they saw me. I was in trouble. I put the razor down before I got carried away and shaved the other eyebrow too.

When Mom walked through the front door that evening, the first thing I did was run to her with my hand over my right eye. "Momma, you'll never guess what happened to me today," I announced. "I looked in your mirror, and my eyebrow fell off!" I moved my hand so she could take a good look. Between my tall tale and my goofy appearance, she couldn't help but laugh. Most of the time, a little humor can save the day.

Success Story

Lena Horne, Singer & Actress

Her beautiful voice, elegant stage presence, and winning personality turned her into an immensely popular performer, especially during the forties and fifties. But even glamorous singers and actresses face an uphill battle. Helena Mary Calhoun Horne knew separation early in life when her father left the family. She was only three years old. With her mother traveling extensively as a theater actress, Lena was raised mainly by her grandparents during her formative years. From the age of seven on she traveled with her mother, which meant that she went from one school to another, never staying in one place long enough to establish lasting friendships.

Despite her incredible talent, she had to struggle her way up in her career at a time when equality hadn't yet been reached. She saw roles go to other actresses, and sometimes her scenes were cut out of movies. Still, she pressed on and created successful careers in both music and movies. Lena has appeared in more than twenty films and her songs are featured in more than two dozen albums. Throughout her life she's maintained her grace and dignity, serving as a role model for people everywhere. Now in the later years of her life, she continues to embrace life fully with an open mind and a courageous heart, as evidenced by her quote, "I'm still learning, you know. At eighty, I feel there is a lot I don't know."

CHAPTER 3
Fear Of Being Exposed

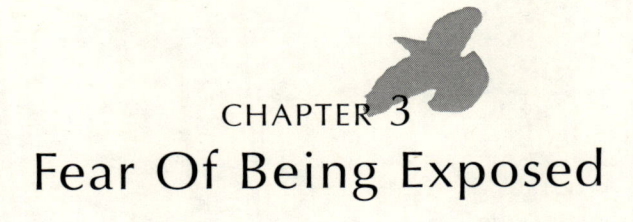

So do not fear, for I am with you;
do not be dismayed, for I am your God.
I will strengthen you and help you;
I will uphold you with my righteous right hand.

the Bible,
New International Version,
Isaiah 41:10

Fear Of Being Exposed

"You gonna make us read today?"

My middle school teacher stopped writing on the board and turned to look at me over her glasses. "Not today, Aldric. Why?"

"No reason," I lied, feeling a sense of relief. "So what'd you think of the president's State of the Union address?"

Knowing how much she loved politics, I made sure to bring up current events every day. I learned that if I could engage my teachers in thought-provoking conversations, they'd like me, and my grade would move up from a D to a C. Talking about their favorite subjects was my way of showing them that I really was smart. Because when it came to reading, I was failing.

> No passion so effectually robs the mind of all its powers of acting and reasoning as fear.
>
> *Edmund Burke*

Mom had no idea I struggled. Every day she asked, "Did you do your homework? Did you get it done?" If I said yes, that was the end of it. If I said not yet, Mom simply stated, "You need to get it done."

I hated going to the war zone that was John F. Kennedy Middle School, where I had to defend myself constantly. I begged to go elsewhere, but my pleas fell on deaf ears. The students at JFK were uncontrollable, intense fighting broke out every day, and most of the teachers lacked motivation. In my mind, the only reason some had become teachers in the first place was to get summers and all those other holidays off. My sister and I fought the tough kids almost daily. We never started these fights, but our nice clothes made us convenient targets, and we weren't about to stand there and take it.

Before going to middle school, I scored extremely low on my assessments and was labeled a "slow learner." Any kid deemed either a slow learner or a bad kid going into JFK didn't stand a chance. Teachers felt they didn't have time to babysit these "problem" kids. As one of the slow learners fighting the bad kids, I desperately sought a teacher who'd stand by me.

Fear Of Being Exposed

> If someone comes to you entreating aid, do not say in refusal: "Trust in God; He will help," but act as if they are an angel.

Nobody did, except for Mr. Perry, the school police officer who was my dad away from home. He was the only person who really looked out for me during those chaotic middle school years. On "Career Day," I chose to explore being a police officer just so I could tag along with Mr. Perry. We were quite a sight, his towering six-foot-three frame and my small four-foot-five build walking side by side down the halls. I was so proud to be helping him that I felt bigger than anyone. In his quiet, subtle way, he encouraged me and kept me on the straight and narrow. To this day I speak with him and thank him for taking the time to talk to me when I was just a middle school kid.

Behind The Cafeteria

To the world, Mr. Perry was just one person. To me, he was the world. He treated me like I was *someone*. To pretty much the rest of the school, though, I was a slow learner nobody had time for. I tried my best to blend in with the crowd. One of the tricks I used was volunteering at the cafeteria. After the bell, I waited until all the kids left the lunchroom to go to their regular classes. Once the coast was clear, I snuck out to the portable buildings behind the cafeteria where classes for slow learners were held.

My classmates and I made a pact with each other:

Not a word to anyone. I'm sure you've heard the phrase, "What happens in Vegas, stays in Vegas." Well, our motto was the same: "Whatever happens in special ed, stays in special ed. If you tell, I tell!" None of us dared spill the beans about somebody else's struggles in the portable classrooms. We knew better. *If you dare tell anyone that I can't read, then I'm gonna tell them something about you that's ten times worse, you can bet on it.* Nobody broke our pact without suffering severe repercussions.

> You can discover what your enemy fears most by observing the means he uses to frighten you.
>
> *Eric Hoffer*

In my regular classes, I used humor and trouble-making to my advantage. Whenever a teacher asked me to read aloud, I cracked jokes to get out of reading. If this didn't work, I purposely did something to get in trouble and out of class. At the principal's office, I then used my mouth, charm, and wit to get out of getting into trouble. I played quite a complicated game just to avoid being exposed.

At that point in my life I still didn't know who I really was. I kept looking to others for my own identity, learning from their example, taking a piece of them and making it a part of me. I hadn't yet developed my own character. Fear was a dominant factor in my decision-making process. Fear of being exposed. Fear of teachers finding out I couldn't read. Fear of kids finding out I had classes in the portable buildings. Unfortunately this fear, which I now regard as "False Evidence Appearing Real," held me back. It kept me from seeking the help I desperately needed to get ahead in school.

New Beginnings

It wasn't until I said goodbye to JFK and entered North Shore High School that I started to discover who I was. Known as the "pretty boy school," North Shore was definitely a better fit. My fighting days diminished considerably. Most of the kids here didn't want to fight me; they wanted to *be* like me. Or at least look like me, because they liked the stylish way I dressed. I joined the Gentlemen's Club; the whole point of our existence was to dress up in a tie once a week and present ourselves as gentlemen. Girls around town liked North Shore guys, because they thought we were cool.

> No great improvements in the lot of mankind are possible until a great change takes place in the fundamental constitution of their modes of thought.
>
> *John Stuart Mill*

I continued to attend SLD (slow learning disability) English classes. Just like in middle school, they were held out of sight in small, stuffy portable buildings behind the cafeteria, but I decided I was tired of that. As a sophomore I made up my mind to do whatever it took to learn to read well so I could get better grades and get out of the portables. My fear of being exposed diminished, and

I started to get help. I made alliances with people willing to assist me. By my junior year, my report cards began to reflect improvement.

Part of the reason I decided to get help was my own embarrassment. As a sophomore I hated being paired up with young freshmen in reading class, and I hated not being able to read above a fifth grade level. It was humiliating. But I also have to give some of the credit for my newfound resolve to my reading teacher, the late Ms. Contrail. She was even shorter than me (I still hadn't had my growth spurt), standing only four feet, two inches tall and that was with heels! She drove an enormous van that was way too big for her, but no matter how funny she looked hopping down from the driver's seat you never, ever laughed at her, because she was a stern, commanding person. Ms. Contrail took me under her wing and taught me that *I can* do this work... if I apply myself.

"In the same way that you're getting people to like you through your charm and your wit," she explained in a matter of fact tone, "you can learn how to read at your grade level." Maybe she was right. I forced myself to read. I didn't like it, but I forced myself to do it.

> It is through suffering that learning comes.
> *Aeschylus*

Once some of that fear of being exposed faded, I learned something very valuable. I learned that when you're willing to open yourself up and admit that you need help, people come out of the woodwork to help you.

I realized they were there all along, waiting for me to be ready to accept their assistance.

Taking Bad Advice

As a kid, I loved baseball with tremendous passion. With my strong throwing arm and right-fielder expertise, I made it on the varsity baseball team as a ninth grader, which was a very big deal. The varsity experience could have taken me somewhere. Making it to varsity that early meant I'd be slotted to get into a league right after high school. Unfortunately, I listened to a dose of bad advice.

"Baseball isn't for blacks, son," one of the coaches told me. "You need to be playing football."

My heart sank. Was this true? I started to pay more attention to baseball on TV. The coach seemed right: It looked like only white guys played pro baseball. Despite my extraordinary skills, it seemed I didn't stand a chance.

> Beware of unsolicited advice.
>
> *Akiba*

I did something I've regretted ever since. I quit baseball, my passion, based on one coach's comments. I never played again. Nobody tried to talk me out of my decision. I think Mom was actually relieved, since she always worried I'd get hurt playing sports.

Giving up baseball was one of the toughest decisions I've ever made. Afterwards I watched the school games, but seeing players out there who weren't half as good as me made the experience almost intolerable. I never made a stink about it, though. As the youngest in my family, I had always been taught to be happy with what I had.

After saying goodbye to baseball I tried my hand at football. Big mistake. I was way too small to be a football player. The other guys mowed me over as if I was a cardboard cutout. So as a sophomore, I quit sports altogether.

Gainful Employment

Alpheaus played football. I made myself his team's official water boy, putting to good use the go-cart I'd won from Burger King one summer. I drove that cart to school as if it was a real car, even though there was nothing else like it on the road. My head stuck way out above its open-air pseudo roof. The doors were soldered into place and didn't open at all, so I had to climb in and out through the top. Boy, was I a sight in that unusual contraption!

On the football field, I loaded up the water, delivered it to the team using my go-kart, and hung out with the guys for a while. After finishing my water boy duties, I got back in my go-cart, returned supplies to the locker room, and drove home. I did this every football practice for four years until my brother graduated from high school.

> From everyone who has been given much, much will be demanded; and from the one who has been entrusted with much, much more will be asked.
>
> *Luke* 12:48 NIV

I took pride in doing a good job for the team. This sense of pride that came from having a responsibility and giving it my best carried over into my very first job as a busboy at the Days Inn Hotel Restaurant. Working opened up a whole new world for me. Suddenly I had money in my pocket. Maybe other guys were smarter, but I had gainful employment. Working made me feel rich.

From the Days Inn, I moved up to bussing tables at another local restaurant, but despite the slightly higher pay it wasn't a change for the better. I absolutely hated working there. Trying to save a few bucks on pest control, the owners limited spraying for roaches to just once a month. Instead they made us busboys clean off every last little crumb from the floor. Every night after closing I spent hours cleaning up, and I never got home before two in the morning. Mom wasn't happy about that. It wasn't long before I quit.

My favorite job was working for Alamo Rent A Car, which I'd earned through sheer persistence. I applied at sixteen and called back every day to check on the status of my application. I kept calling and calling the manager until the day he told me to come in and fill out paperwork because the job was mine. I began to see that persistence is the key to unlocking any door you want to open.

> Whoever knocks persistently, ends by entering.
>
> *Ali*

My job was to fill each returned rental car with gas, vacuum it, and drive it to the back where others did the washing and detailing. I loved it. And the pay was good, too. Unfortunately, after four weeks at Alamo I received bad news.

"Aldric, I'm sorry to tell you that we're going to have to let you go," my manager informed me.

"Why?" I asked, taken aback. "Haven't I been doing a good job?"

"Oh yes, you've been doing a fantastic job! But I just noticed on your application that you're only sixteen. You're too young to be driving our cars. You're a great worker, Aldric. I want you to come back when you're eighteen, okay?"

Working gave me self-esteem. It made me feel that I truly was in control. I put in my best effort, moved ahead in life, and made some money. With a job, I was on a schedule where somebody depended on me to perform specific tasks. People needed me. Not to mention, I had spending money for movies, clothes, and gas for my car. It felt good.

Friends, Fun, & Responsibility

Perhaps because I was the last one on the totem pole, Mom seemed to fuss over my brother and sister more than she did over me. Alpheus got brand name shirts, but by the time we got to shopping for me the money always ran out, and I got whatever was on sale. Erica got emotional support, while I got, "Don't be late, you hear?" Today Mom tells me that I didn't need as much help as they did. That may be true, but back then I felt I was getting the short end of the deal, and it frustrated me greatly. I did get something out of it, though. I learned to be independent and take care of my own needs. I learned to take responsibility for myself.

> The greatest thing in the world is to know how to belong to oneself.
>
> *Montaigne*

Part of being independent and responsible means doing your own chores. Like laundry, for example. I started doing my own laundry out of necessity when I was pretty young. We had a lot of wildlife around our house, especially alligators. My friends and I liked to go fishing and hunting rabbits early Saturday mornings. All of us were allowed to do these things, but we weren't allowed to get up on an old wooden dock in the midst of alligator country. Our moms considered it too dangerous. I didn't see what the problem was since I was an excellent swimmer.

My buddies and I decided to fish from that dock in the murky, alligator-infested water. Who ended up falling off? Me, of course. Down I went into the deep water thick with mud and green slime. Swimming here wasn't so easy, I discovered. I quickly made a plan. I would sink to the bottom and then push off with my feet to reach the surface.

Suddenly I felt someone grab me. It was my good friend Kevin Pierson. He pulled me out of the murky depths and helped me to the shore. I thanked him for jumping in and saving me.

I hurried home and threw all my wet clothes into the dryer. Once they were dry, I put them back on. That night, when it was time for my bath, I left my clothing in the dirty clothes hamper. Mom took one look at the hamper and asked me, "What's going on here?" My once gleaming white underwear and T-shirt were no longer white. I had dried the dirty, muddy water into my underclothes. That day Mom decided it was high time I learned to wash clothes properly. I've been doing it ever since, and I'm proud to say that today I can get even the most ground-in stain out. By the way, I did get a whooping for disobeying and going to that old dock.

> A real friend never gets in your way unless you happen to be on your way down.
>
> *Anonymous*

In high school I had a number of close friends, many of whom are still good friends of mine. My next-door neighbor, Joe Preston, and I would sit in front of our houses together and watch the cars pass by. Keith Reid, the preacher's son, would come over on weekends and we'd spend all day at our pool. Bobby Jones was like a brother to me; later I became the best man at his wedding. During my junior year he and I and a few other friends drove off to watch a basketball tournament three hours away and spent the night there, without first telling our parents. We definitely got in trouble for that. Then there was Bryan Boysaw, my brother's friend who quickly became my best friend and now I call him my older brother. Like me he was the youngest of three children, so we had a lot in common. Two years older than me, Bryan watched out for me. He made sure I was included in whatever the other guys did.

Time and again, I was the designated driver. That's because I didn't like to drink. Dad had helped rid me of any desire or curiosity I might have had about drinking. It wasn't pleasant; I hope the rest of you have the wisdom to stay away from alcohol without having to learn your lesson like I did.

One Saturday afternoon Dad invited several friends over, and they sat around talking and drinking sherry. At fifteen I wanted to be a big man, so I asked if I could try the sherry. He gave me a taste. I came back later and asked for more. He gave me a little more. I came back again, and again. After the fourth time, I could no longer stand up or walk straight. I did not like how the alcohol had taken control of my body.

> A moment's insight is sometimes worth a life's experience.
>
> *Oliver Wendell Holmes*

That evening, my family and I went out to dinner at Morrison's Cafeteria. A long line of people waited to get inside. As I stood in that line, I started to feel sick. I excused myself, went into the restroom, and threw up. I went back out and asked Mom if I could wait in the car. There, I fell asleep.

Next thing I knew, Mom was waking me up for church. I'd missed dinner, and I didn't even remember getting back home. Mom drew open the drapes. Blinding sunlight poured in, making my hangover headache hurt even more. From that moment on, I decided I wouldn't let anything take control of my body. No alcohol, no drugs. That's how I became the designated driver for my friends. Whenever we went out to a restaurant or club, I danced, I ate, and I had a soda or two, but I never drank alcohol. Still don't. And I know I'm not missing a thing.

Love Of My Life

When I went to football games and other school events, I liked to wear cowboy boots, jeans, and my blue denim jacket. I guess dressing up like a cowboy did the trick, because a really cute girl named Kim noticed me. I was a junior, she was a freshman, and at first, I didn't even realize that this beauty from another school was checking me out.

My good friend Carl Foster had a crush on Kim, so you can imagine how excited he was when she spotted him at the park one Sunday afternoon and walked straight to him. As Kim looked into his eyes, his heart beat faster and his hopes rose astronomically.

"Carl, would you do me a favor?" she asked sweetly.

He was thrilled beyond imagination. "Yes, Kim," he answered earnestly. "You know I'll do anything for you. Just say the word."

"Would you introduce me to Aldric?"

> Build a team of positive people around you, and your connection to the world will soon open up.

His heart dropped. All his hoping and dreaming vanished into thin air. Managing a half-hearted smile, Carl replied, "Yeah, sure, I'll introduce you to him."

That's how Kim and I met, and before long before we decided we'd like to date each other. I wanted to do things right, the old-fashioned way. So I met her mother, Mrs. Ferguson, and asked, "May I date your daughter?"

That swept her off her feet. Nobody had ever asked for permission before. Mrs. Ferguson gave her approval. Kim and I started dating, and I began to discover what a fun, caring, and compassionate person she is. She learned of my academic struggles, and she never ceased to encourage me. Kim and her family were tremendously positive role models for me. That family showed me what being together is. I have never, ever heard Kim's parents argue, and they're together to this day.

Being young, with our whole future still ahead of us, we dated on and off during those high school years. During one of the "off" periods, Kim started dating my friend Bobby Red. I warned him, "If you ever mess up, she's as good as gone." He messed up. His loss was my gain, because Kim and I started dating again, and our courtship eventually led to marriage. This year we celebrated our sixteenth anniversary. Bobby Red and I are still good friends, and every so often I thank him for messing up, and in return he half jokes that he wishes he hadn't messed up.

Graduation Day

I made it through the rest of high school by keeping my eye on the prize: a diploma in my hand on graduation day. My brother and sister had received their high school diplomas, and I knew I had to get mine, too. If I didn't, it was clear to me I'd be at a huge disadvantage my entire life. Besides, I knew Mom expected me to graduate. It would give her bragging rights around her friends. Not every mother in my neighborhood could say that all of her children had graduated from high school.

> Perseverance is the hard work you do after you get tired of doing the hard work you already did.
>
> *Newt Gingrrich*

I worked hard. Really hard. Through sheer persistence and determination, I reached a level that allowed me to get out of special education and into regular classes exclusively. I was proud of this accomplishment. By no means was I at the top of my classes (with the possible exception of shop class where I enjoyed working with wood and building with my hands), but just *making* it into these classes was quite a feat for me. I worked doubly hard and somehow, I made it. I fulfilled my academic requirements. On graduation day, I had my diploma in hand. I graduated from high school with a 2.0 GPA. Mom could brag.

Some of my friends were headed for college. Others went to work right away. As for me, Lackland Air Force Base in San Antonio, Texas was my next stop. Suddenly, it was a whole new ballgame.

Success Story

Charles Schwab, Businessman, Entrepreneur & CEO

Many people know that Charles Robert Schwab, Jr. is the founder and CEO of the brokerage house Charles Schwab Corporation. But what a lot of folks don't know is that he's always struggled with reading and writing. School was painfully difficult for him. Charles was good in math, science, and sports, but he had to fake it when it came to English. He always asked himself, "Why am I slower than the other kids in class?" It wasn't until about twenty years ago that he realized he has dyslexia.

To this day, reading requires great effort for Charles, but he's learned strategies to help him overcome his learning disability. Over the years, he also grew in other skills as he compensated for the areas that were difficult for him. He developed strong leadership, entrepreneurial, and managerial abilities, which, of course, serve him well as CEO.

Remembering the embarrassment and challenges he experienced regularly during his school years, Charles has chosen to help youngsters who struggle as he has. He and his wife Helen help children with learning disabilities through their private foundation, which has launched such programs as Schwab Learning and its associated website, SchwabLearning.org. This successful business leader has taken action so that young people with learning disabilities can have an easier, more enjoyable experience in school and become enthusiastic lifelong learners.

CHAPTER 4
My Brief Air Force Stint

United we stand; divided we fall.

Aesop,
ancient Greek fabulist

My Brief Air Force Stint

"Don't worry, men, we'll take good care of you," the sergeant assured us new recruits on the bus ride from the airport to Lackland Air Force Base. "Right off the bat, you'll get twenty-four hours of sleep so you'll be well-rested when training begins."

We were so green we believed him. Young, fresh faces from across the country were on that bus, representing all colors and ethnicities. It was June of 1986, one month away from my eighteenth birthday, and I was excited to begin my next adventure. Alpheus was in the Army, but this time I didn't follow him. I chose the Air Force because of my fascination with airplanes and my dream of flying.

> Be not afraid of life. Believe that life is worth living, and your belief will help create the fact.
>
> *William James*

The bus pulled into the base, and we stepped off, eager to begin our six weeks of Basic Military Training. There we stood, forty guys in my platoon, holding our bags and waiting for instructions. Sergeant Thompson, our training instructor, stood before us with a scowl on his face. Tall and muscular, he looked like he was trying extra hard to come across as mean.

"Drop your bags!" he commanded.

Surprised, we did as told. He shook his head. "Pathetic," he assessed. "Pick them up. *Drop Them!*"

Once again we did what he commanded, not knowing why we were doing this but knowing that we had better obey, or else. We had our personal bags from home, each one with a metallic piece running along the bottom. When we dropped our bags, you could hear a series of clicks as the metal from each bag hit the concrete. Looking disgusted, our sergeant finally explained his goal.

"On my command, you will drop your bags immediately. All of the bags will hit the ground at precisely the same moment, creating one unified sound. Understood? Drop them!"

Click, click, click, click. Completely out of synch.

My Brief Air Force Stint

> If a task once begun never leave it till it's done. Be the labor great or small, Do it well or not at all.
>
> *Anonymous*

We stood there for hours dropping our bags. Over, and over, and over again we let go upon his order. Slowly we made progress. Finally we achieved one large unified click followed by a slight echo click from those whose reflexes were slower. Unfortunately, this wasn't good enough for Sergeant Thompson. The sun had set hours ago, and it was well past midnight. Would this exercise ever end?

Finally, at two in the morning, we did it. Upon our training instructor's command, we dropped our bags. *Click!* One loud unified sound. No stray clicks whatsoever. I couldn't believe my ears. Exhausted, we filed into our barracks and soon fell asleep.

It felt like we'd just closed our eyes when we awoke with a start to loud banging and shouting. What the heck was going on? We looked at our watches. It was five o'clock in the morning, for goodness' sakes! We could barely hear Reveille playing outside, because inside our sleeping quarters, officers made a deafening racket beating on trash lids. With less than three hours of sleep, we were groggy and confused. Our complaints were answered with shouts and commands that made us quickly realize we'd been tricked. Scared, we stopped our complaining and did as we were told.

We met our daytime training instructor, Sergeant Fulcrum, who was shorter than Sergeant Thompson and not quite as loud. He yelled instructions, and we marched off to get our military haircuts. I was ahead of the game here. In preparation, I had already gotten a haircut. They weren't going to shave *my* head.

I was wrong. "Hey, I just got my hair cut," I complained over the sound of electric razors going full blast. "Why do I gotta get it cut again?"

"Everybody gets their hair cut," the barber snapped back. "I don't care if you're bald; you're still getting your hair cut. We're all the same now. We're a team, a family."

> Don't complain. The people who will listen can't do anything about it, while the people who can do something about it won't listen.
>
> *John M. Hebert*

Next we got our clothes. We were like cattle being herded down the line. Someone handed me a pair of boots, size ten. Now, I was still a pretty small guy (my growth spurt didn't arrive until later that year) and my feet were only a size seven.

"I can't wear these," I complained. "They're way too big!"

"Keep moving down the line, son."

Next they handed me a shirt, extra large. Again I complained, and I asked for a medium. Again I got the same answer.

"Just keep going, son. Keep moving down the line."

One piece at a time, we received our uniform and other military clothing. Before long I realized why we got such oversized clothes. As part of Basic Military Training

(BMT), we marched. And marched. And marched some more. With all that walking, we developed huge blisters on our feet. We needed oversized shoes for the simple reason that our swollen, blistered feet needed that extra room.

When I finally had a brief moment to myself, I called Kim. I hadn't told her I was joining the military, nor had I said bye. I just can't handle goodbyes; they tear me up. I much prefer to leave it at "see you later." So instead, I sent her a note when I left for the Air Force, letting her know I'd call the first chance I got.

"Where are you?" she asked.

"I'm in the military."

A Unified Front

As new recruits, we were the absolute lowest on the totem pole. We didn't even get our names on our uniforms until after three weeks had passed. There was no getting around it every other airman *knew* you were a new recruit. When we weren't marching, we had our noses stuck in books. Even when we stood in the chow line, we were expected to study. We stood in a straight line, heel to toe, with our BMT manuals "the Air Force bible," in hand, studying furiously. The manual taught us everything we needed to know, from what to say to what we were expected to do to information we'd be tested on.

As we stood there reading, we were supposed to be as quiet as monks who'd taken a vow of silence. No talking whatsoever. And definitely no laughing.

> You have to laugh sometimes to keep from crying.
>
> *Anonymous*

Unfortunately, one of my new friends started to laugh. His laughter was contagious, and I couldn't help it; I began to laugh, too, even though I tried hard to hold it down. I glanced at Sergeant Fulcrum to see if he had noticed. His angry red face told me that he had. He stomped over to me and stopped inches from my face, where his fury exploded. "What you laughing at, boy?" I had never before encountered such an attack of rage. And I never again laughed in the chow line.

Funny thing was, despite being scared and uncertain, I felt like I fit in. We were all in the same boat, all of us frightened and wondering what we'd gotten ourselves into. And because we were all in this together, we quickly formed a strong bond with each other.

Even with Psycho. I don't remember his real name, but that's what all of us called him. He couldn't do a darn thing. He was the reason we had to drop our bags until two in the morning that first night. Psycho was the very last person to get in sync. He couldn't march. If everybody started with their left foot, he'd start with his right. This skinny, clumsy white kid couldn't even shave. Granted, he had no facial hair, but in the Air Force all of us were required to shave every day regardless. The first time he tried, he cut up his face so badly that he walked out with about fifty tiny pieces of toilet paper plastered across his mug to stop the bleeding. He seemed hopeless.

> Success is a team not an individual.

But he wasn't. Psycho became everyone's friend precisely because he needed our help, and our platoon needed him to shape up. He became our personal project. Everyone pulled in to help him, partly because we felt sorry for the guy and partly because the success of our group depended on every man doing his job right. Whenever he messed up, all of us were penalized.

The first thing we did was show Psycho how to shave. It worked. After his second try, only twenty-five pieces of toilet paper covered his face. The next day, it went down to fifteen tiny pieces. Eventually, he was able to shave without cutting himself, and those little toilet paper bits became a thing of the past.

Next we worked on marching. With every misstep Psycho took, the whole platoon was forced to march more miles. We'd had enough of that, so we took him aside and taught him his left from his right, and we practiced shouting out commands while a couple of us marched with him. Soon, he got it. Not only could he march, he even had a little rhythm in him.

> The reason why the world lacks unity, and lies broken and in heaps, is because man is disunited with himself.
>
> *Ralph Waldo Emerson*

Unity. That's what Air Force Basic Training was about for us. We learned how to be a united family. Everyone made friends with everyone else in the platoon, regardless of what color we were or how we spoke or what part of the country we came from. We were all brothers united with a common goal, a joint purpose. I felt a strong camaraderie with everyone in my platoon. We all needed each other, and we all helped each other. It wasn't about one person being better than the rest. It was about becoming one heart, one mind, one soul. If someone slowed down while jogging, someone else would pull him along. If someone fell behind in any way, others would come to his side and say, "Don't worry, we'll help you. You'll get there. We'll do it together." It was all about family unity.

Goodbye, Air Force

I was doing so well that I quickly became platoon leader. I never got a demerit, never was seriously reprimanded. I caught on quickly, and I fit in better than I ever had in all my years at school.

To get into the Air Force, I had to take an entrance exam during my senior year in high school. It was a very challenging test covering math, reading, logic, even some sections on mechanics, electronics, and other specialties. The test was timed, with monitors walking up and down rows, staring students down to make sure nobody cheated. It was very intimidating. I passed, just barely.

Once in the Air Force, we were required to take that test again. This time I felt even more intimidated. The words swam before my eyes. I felt distracted and couldn't

My Brief Air Force Stint

focus. In the end, I failed the test by two points. This meant that I had to leave the Air Force.

"Come On Back Home, Son"

I had no desire whatsoever to leave. The Air Force was right for me. Without a doubt my superiors saw leadership qualities in me, otherwise they would not have made me platoon leader. I had so much potential. It made no sense. I wanted to be here, but I wasn't allowed, while other guys who wanted out were forced to stay. A young man had recently gone AWOL. After missing for two days, he was found hiding five miles away. They dragged him back and forced him to continue. On the other hand I *wanted* to stay, but I couldn't. It didn't seem right.

> U-turns are common in life. It allows you to get back on track.

I called Mom and gave her the bad news. "I didn't pass the test, Mom." As those words came out of my mouth, I wondered, *what next?* Should I try my luck in California? Or Connecticut maybe, where I knew some relatives? Some other place?

"Just come on back home, son," I heard Mom say. There was no trace of anger in her tone. Only compassion and understanding.

My last day with the Air Force was bittersweet. As Sergeant Fulcrum and I said our goodbyes, I couldn't hold back. "It's a shame that those of us who want to make a difference in society have to leave," I stated, "while those who don't want to be here are forced to stay."

I could see sadness and regret in the sergeant's eyes. "You're right, we need people like you in here," he spoke from his heart. "If I had a whole platoon with people like you, my job would be easy. We'd have the best team."

We shook hands. He wished me luck, and I flew back home.

Hanging On To Dreams

One of the reasons I enlisted with the Air Force was a bigger dream I had: to work for a large aerospace firm in Florida. I figured that serving with the Air Force would boost my chances of eventually getting a job there. Well, "eventually" came sooner than expected. It was time to go after that dream.

> When a man stops dreaming... that man stops living.

My brief time with the Air Force taught me much. In just a few weeks I had experienced tremendous personal growth. I'd become self-reliant and focused on what I had to do to succeed. With one door closed, I wanted to prove to myself that when I came to the next door of opportunity, I would do whatever it took to succeed. I didn't see my brief stint with the military as a failure. I saw it as part of my experience of self-development.

My Brief Air Force Stint

Returning to Florida with greater determination, I set out to get a job with my dream company.

Six weeks later, I reached my goal. I was offered a job at the aerospace company. My dream came true... more or less. I couldn't get a position in the stockroom or the engine room, like I wanted. So I accepted a position in their scrap yard.

Success Story

Curtis Sliwa, Social Activist & Defender of the Peace

This New Yorker has always taken it upon himself to make his community a better, cleaner, and safer place for everyone. Kicked out of high school during his senior year for his student activism, Curtis Sliwa declined a scholarship to Brown University and instead continued his work as a grassroots activist. Working as a manager at a fast food restaurant, Curtis (who was raised in a tight-knit Polish-Italian Christian family) organized efforts to clean up graffiti and plant trees throughout his community.

He went on to recruit volunteers of all cultural backgrounds and ethnicities to patrol a crime-ridden subway line in his neighborhood. Through the power of citizen's arrests, these volunteers—who initially met considerable resistance from authorities—were able to round up criminals and detain them for the police. This effort grew in both the number of volunteers and the areas patrolled, evolving into The Guardian Angels, which Curtis founded.

He's taken his peaceful surveillance tactics internationally, with his organization expanding beyond New York into dozens of U.S. cities and eleven countries, including England, Japan, South Africa, Peru, and New Zealand. This growth is even more remarkable when you consider that over the years The Guardian Angels faced a great deal of opposition from numerous camps, including New York's mayor at the time, Ed Koch (later on, he changed his opinion, becoming a supporter of the organization). Curtis has been shot by the Mafia, and two of his Guardian Angels have been killed while on duty.

Nevertheless, he remains committed to combating violence and keeping the peace through unarmed citizen crime patrollers. Membership has grown from the original thirteen New Yorkers to more than five thousand people around the world. In addition to keeping streets safe, The Guardian Angels visit schools and businesses to teach about nonviolence and safety. Curtis shows how one concerned citizen can start a neighborhood movement that ultimately improves the health and safety of urban communities everywhere.

CHAPTER 5
"You'll Never Leave The Scrap Yard!"

The difference between the impossible and the possible lies in a person's determination.

Tommy Lasorda,
Major League baseball pitcher, manager

"You'll Never Leave The Scrap Yard!"

The aerospace firm's five acres of scrap yard were littered with dismantled engines and miscellaneous airplane parts. In the midst of this metallic graveyard stood a small shack, our only shelter from the beating sun, driving rains, and unrelenting mosquitoes. Three of us worked here. Our job was to process heaps of metal, separating what was salvageable from the junk. We were modern-day prospectors digging for titanium, nickel, and gold.

We sorted these metals into three large bins. Whenever we ran across a part whose metal composition was in question, we placed it inside a large machine, added liquid nitrogen (which we made sure *never* to touch because it would mean instant frostbite), and waited for a reading. If the machine told us the part was mostly nickel, that's the bin it went into. By and large, though, we sorted by sight. Some of the scrap came to us in large, fifty-five-gallon drums we had to sift through.

> The job maybe thoughtless, but the experience is worth the pay.

It had to be the most boring job in the world. Not to mention, it was stifling hot in the yard. I *knew* I never wanted to set foot in hell, because if it was hot like this scrap yard I wanted no part of it! I don't know how we were expected to complete full eight-hour shifts under these conditions, but we were. So the three of us devised a plan. We decided to give ourselves extended breaks to cool off and avoid heat exhaustion.

During our breaks one of us stayed outside in the yard as the lookout while the other two cooled off in the shack drinking water and resting. We took turns serving as lookout. In this manner we were able to meet our quota for the day without killing ourselves under the intense sun.

Because the job was so mindless, I started picking up magazines covering everything from world news to travel to modern science to keep my mind occupied. I read them during my long breaks. My reading skills were still poor, but here in the scrap yard I wasn't self-conscious about it. With my lookout watching for supervisors and my other coworker fast asleep, I could sit and read safely, in private, for long stretches at a time. Whenever I didn't understand something, I read it over and over and over again until I got it. There was no pressure, no teacher looking over my shoulder, no worries about having to read aloud in front of my peers.

Slowly my reading skills improved. Little by little, it just got easier for me. After several months, I realized that an amazing thing was happening at that scrap yard. I was discovering my love of reading.

The Power Of Books

In high school, I avoided reading like the plague. It was a source of constant embarrassment and frustration. But here in this tiny shack, reading opened up a whole new world for me. It became apparent that I could read a book, and it would transport me to far-off places. I wasn't in the boiling scrap yard anymore. I was riding a Venetian gondola in Italy or scuba diving in Australia's Great Barrier Reef or hearing the surf crash in a California beach. With a rush of excitement I realized that even if I never got to visit these places in person, I could always pick up a book and "be there."

Then I discovered motivational books, and there was no turning back. I picked up *Success Journey* by John C. Maxwell. Never in my life had I read a book from cover to cover the way I devoured this one. When Dr. Maxwell gave a talk at my church, I asked him to sign my copy (by the way, he's now assistant pastor there). After I read his book, something inside me clicked. I got hooked on self-help books. I began to read everything on the subject I could get my hands on. And I wondered, *why didn't I learn any of this important stuff in school or in the Air Force?*

I began to make plans for myself. I decided I'd been

at the scrap yard long enough, and I was getting myself out. It was time to move up.

> When you decide to take on a challenge, always remember to act as if it was impossible to fail.
>
> *Isaiah Fleurimond*

"What Makes You Think You Can Get Out?"

I shared my goal with my coworkers. They laughed. The scrap yard was their day-to-day reality. They'd been there three, maybe four years, and despite their complaints and the awful work conditions, they seemed content enough to remain there. Their motto was "retire or die in the scrap yard."

"We've been here all these years," they chided, "and there haven't been any promotions for us. What makes *you* think you can get out? No, Aldric, you're not gonna get out of here."

They weren't saying this out of meanness or a sense of jealousy. It was nothing like that. The plain truth was that they were trapped. As much as they disliked the blistering heat, as much as they complained about the drudgery of their jobs, something was holding them back. Something kept them from trying to get ahead. It was fear, plain and simple, that kept them trapped in the scrap yard. So they sat there, week after week, year after year, taking what was dished out to them by the elements and by the supervisor, because they were afraid to do what they had to do in order to get out of that place.

"You'll Never Leave The Scrap Yard!"

> Everybody is ambitious. The question is whether you are ambitious to be or ambitious to do.
>
> *Jean Monnet*

Not me. I was at my dream company, but this definitely was not my dream job. A year at the yard was more than enough for me. I put in a request to transfer to another department. It was promptly denied. *No problem,* I thought, *I'll keep looking.* Every week I checked the job listings posted at the company. Then one day, I found it: an opening in shipping and receiving. Definitely a step up from the scrap yard. I filled out the necessary paperwork and again requested a transfer. This time, I got it!

There was only one small glitch: my new job was in Connecticut.

Doing What It Takes

I didn't tell Kim. I couldn't. Goodbyes were excruciating for me. Besides, this was just temporary. It was not an ideal situation, being away from my girlfriend and all things familiar, but it was what I had to do to move up in the company. Sometimes we have to make small sacrifices to reach bigger rewards.

The company's main hub was in East Hartford, Connecticut. I'd never even been that far north. Labor Day weekend I packed my car, said goodbye to Mom, and with my sister and niece began the long drive up I-95 through Florida, Georgia, the Carolinas, Virginia, DC, Maryland, Delaware, New Jersey, and New York to my new state. Our Connecticut cousins welcomed us with open arms. My sister and her daughter were there just for a visit, while I moved in with our cousins.

> Once you say you're going to settle for second, that's what happens to you in life.
>
> *John F. Kennedy*

There was a lot I didn't know about Connecticut. First, I had no idea how cold it could get there. Second, I didn't realize my cousins lived so far away from my job. None of it mattered, though. I was driven by my desire to get out of the scrap yard and move up in the world. Everything else would fall into place.

I called Kim. "Guess where I am?"

"Where are you, Aldric?"

"I'm in Connecticut."

"What are you doing up there?"

I explained everything to my patient girlfriend. Thank goodness she was understanding. We stayed together, through the distance.

I met wonderful people in Connecticut. My cousins were so gracious to me, the way they took me in at their Waterbury home and let me live with them. I had an hour commute every day to work and another hour commute back to my place.

My shift started at 3:30 in the afternoon. I worked hard, kept my nose clean, did my job well. I made several friends, forging a lasting friendship with Darrel Peaks, an ex-Marine who worked in security there at the aircraft facility. A few years older than me, Darrel took me under

"You'll Never Leave The Scrap Yard!"

his wing and showed me the sights in Connecticut. We helped each other whenever we could.

When I wasn't working I loved to explore nearby areas, Boston and New York being two of my favorites. One beautiful Saturday I was driving around Boston when an elderly couple in a huge Cadillac pulled out in front of me and hit my car. Thankfully nobody was hurt, but my car needed fixing. I called Mom and asked if she'd lend me $100 for the insurance deductible, which I'd pay back as soon as I got my check that coming Thursday. I did not want to ask my cousins for the loan. They'd already taken me in and done so much for me.

> If you can't help a person don't hurt them, encourage them.

"Aldric, I'm strapped for cash right now. Why don't you call your father?"

Over the years I had tried to reach out to him, to build a relationship, but Dad kept his distance. Maybe this was another opportunity to reconnect with him. I listened to Mom's suggestion and called my biological dad, who was still living with his mom, reaching him through his personal phone line.

"Don't call me collect no more on my phone," he scolded.

"Dad, I'm sorry, but I need a hundred dollars. It's an emergency. I'll pay you back as soon as I get paid this week."

"I don't have the money. I can't help you. Next time

you want to reach me, call me at your grandma's phone number. She can afford to pay for the call. I can't."

"Okay, Dad, I hear you. You don't have to worry about me anymore."

That was the last time I tried to connect with my biological father. I also decided that from that point on, I wouldn't ask Mom for anything anymore.

I called my girlfriend. "Kim, I got in a minor car accident. I'm fine, but I need a hundred dollars for the deductible. Can you send it over? I'll pay you right back later this week when I get paid."

She was working at a department store, making a very modest income. But she saw it in her heart to send me the money, enabling me to get my car fixed up. Kim got me out of a jam. And I paid her right back, like I promised.

Too Cold For Me

My while in Connecticut was a time of growth and independence. I met new people, saw new places, and was given new responsibilities at work. I started to really rely on myself and grow up on many levels. There were only a few minor hiccups now and then, like the time someone pulled up beside me as I was stopped at a traffic light.

"Hey man, you got some stuff?" he leaned out and asked. Stuff? What the heck was he talking about? "Got any marijuana?" the guy clarified.

I was livid. "I don't do that," I yelled back. "I work hard for a living, and I don't do that stuff. Don't *ever* approach me with that mess anymore!"

I later shared this encounter with my cousins. "You

know what?" one said. "I'm pretty sure that was an undercover police officer. You're a new face in town. They were just checking you out, making sure you weren't pushing drugs or anything." I calmed down. If it was an officer, then it wasn't so bad. He was just doing his job.

From September through January, things went rather smoothly. Then came February, bringing the nastiest, coldest weather I'd ever experienced. I had to learn quickly how to drive in snow. I hated it. The blizzard conditions made for awful commutes. I didn't like how the salt and sand dumped on the roads to melt the stuff made a mess of my nice car, either.

> Self-sufficiency...has three meanings. The first is that one should not depend upon others for one's daily bread. The second is that one should have developed the power to acquire knowledge for oneself. The third is that a man should be able to rule himself, to control his senses and his thoughts.
>
> *Vinoba Bhave*

One day I couldn't stand how dirty my car had gotten, so I took it to the carwash. Little did I know that temperatures were to drop below freezing that night. Around midnight, after ending my shift at work, I tried to get into my car to begin the long drive across treacherous roads back home. I tried unlocking the door, but my key wouldn't go in. I grabbed the door handle and pulled. Nothing happened. I tried again and again, alternating between the key that wouldn't go in and the handle that wouldn't budge, with no luck. The door was frozen shut.

Apparently water from the carwash had seeped into the window and door, and the cold temperatures froze it solid.

I went back inside the facility and called a friend and coworker. "I can't get in my car. The door's frozen shut! Can you help me?"

He came right over. "Let me have your car key," he said. I handed it over. He took out a cigarette lighter and passed the flame through the key, heating it up. It worked. He managed to get the key in. But the door still wouldn't open. He tugged and pulled to no avail. He peered inside. "There's got to be ice on the inside," he said.

Before I could stop him, he started banging on the door to break the ice. I like to take good care of things and keep them working well and looking good. I inspected my car door and saw a large dent he'd just created. I wasn't happy about that.

But I let it go. After all, without hesitation he'd rushed outside on that bleak, frigid night to bail me out. His unorthodox techniques worked. He got the door open. I thanked him and left for home.

I drove my stick shift in the dark, cold night along I-84 with the heater on full blast to try to fully defrost that door, because even though I could now open it, it wouldn't close shut completely. Something inside was still frozen, and I couldn't latch it closed. The heat was making me drowsy, so I rolled down the windows to let cold air in to keep me awake. The roads were dangerously slick with ice. I prayed the entire way. And I kept asking myself, *What have I got myself into?*

"You'll Never Leave The Scrap Yard!"

> Experience is a hard teacher because she gives the test first, the lesson afterwards.
>
> *Vernon Law*

After a few more bouts with snow and rain, I decided I'd had enough. I requested a transfer, and my request was granted. After putting in a full year at the Connecticut facility, from one September to the next, I packed my belongings, thanked my cousins, and moved back to West Palm Beach, exchanging snow and sleet for palm trees and warm ocean breezes.

Success Story

Mae Jemison, Doctor, Chemical Engineer, Professor & Astronaut

When she was a child, her inquisitive nature was encouraged by her parents. As early as kindergarten Mae Carol Jemison knew she wanted to be a scientist, and she spent much of her childhood exploring nature and studying how things work. She also loved dancing and considered becoming a professional dancer. At the age of sixteen, she headed for Stanford University with a scholarship. There Mae earned her Bachelor of Science degree in Chemical Engineering. She went on to earn her Doctorate in Medicine from Cornell Medical College.

One of her dreams had always been to go into space, and she reached that goal when she went into orbit in NASA's space shuttle in 1992, five years after being chosen for the astronaut program. Aboard the shuttle she served as Science Mission Specialist. In the process of achieving her big dream, Mae became the first black woman in space. She's lived a rich, fulfilling life, both prior to and after reaching this giant accomplishment.

Some of her successes include:

- Serving with the Peace Corps as a medical officer in Africa
- Researching vaccines with the Center for Disease Control

- Working as a general practitioner in California
- Launching her own company, the Jemison Group, which develops science and technology for everyday living
- Appearing in an episode of Star Trek: The Next Generation
- Starting a foundation that offers youth educational programs, including an international science camp
- Producing shows featuring modern jazz and African dance
- Teaching at Dartmouth College
- Being inducted into the National Women's Hall of Fame

Mae shows us that we don't have to restrict ourselves and our dreams. Just because we've chosen one career path doesn't mean others are closed to us. We can follow dreams, follow our heart, and follow our passion to create a unique and highly rewarding life for ourselves. As Mae once said, "Don't let anyone rob you of your imagination, your creativity, or your curiosity. It's your place in the world; it's your life. Go on and do all you can with it, and make it the life you want to live."

CHAPTER 6
Layoffs And Mean Dogs

I can accept failure. Everyone fails at something. But I can't accept not trying.

Michael Jordan

Layoffs And Mean Dogs

"**M**ade it back, huh?" my buddies at the scrap yard greeted me warmly. Yep, I was back where I started, but thankfully *not* at my old job. It took two transfers and two moves to climb up from the insufferable scrap yard to shipping and receiving and finally to aircraft inspection, the department I'd wanted to work at all along. I was reunited with my girlfriend, and I had a great job at my dream company. What more could I want?

My heart went out to the guys in the yard. They were happy to see me move up in the company, but they still couldn't figure out how to do it themselves. Either they didn't know how, or they were too scared to take that uncertain but necessary next step. I hoped that in time, my example would help them take the initiative to advance.

> The best measure of courage is the fear that is overcome.
>
> *Norman F. Dixon*

As an aircraft inspector, I had a ball in the "big house." I worked with talented, creative engineers and technicians. I got to see the latest designs and hear about the newest innovations. I was like a kid in a candy shop! It was absolutely perfect, with one exception: Rumors of more layoffs began to circulate.

The aerospace sector is notorious for having one layoff after another, but it hadn't been that way when I was growing up. Back then it was a solid industry, with layoffs virtually unheard of. That's why some of my high school friends and I wanted to work for this aerospace firm; to us it meant interesting work, good pay, and job security. Things had changed by the time I got there. Every year we were subjected to threats of new layoffs, hearing about it first through the grapevine and later, right around Christmas, directly from supervisors. They'd come by and announce, "There's a good chance we're gonna have layoffs at the start of the year." That always put a damper on the holidays. Nobody dared spend much for Christmas because, come January, they might be out of a job.

I started in the inspection department in September, newest guy aboard and among the youngest on the team. In January, just four months later, my supervisor called me to his office. I knew what was coming.

"I hate to do this," my boss, an older gentleman who'd been there for decades, started, "but I'm gonna have to lay you off." Without saying much else, he handed me my packing papers.

> Man is most uniquely human when he turns obstacles into opportunities.
>
> *Eric Hoffer*

I wasn't the only one getting a pink slip. Other young guys on my team were losing their jobs that day. But my supervisor's friends, many of whom were close to retirement and perhaps *should* have taken early retirement so the rest of us could keep our jobs, were protected. None of them lost their jobs.

I looked straight at my supervisor and, very calmly, replied, "You know what? I'll accept this. But I've got one thing going for me right now that you don't have. I have the opportunity to move forward, to get another job. But here you are, at the age that you are. What are you going to do when they try to lay *you* off? Companies aren't interested in hiring someone your age."

I didn't say this to be mean. I just wanted him to see the truth. I knew he was protecting his buddies (and himself). I'd seen how they were moved out of inspection into other departments; once layoffs were over and the smoke had cleared, he'd bring them right back. I'd watched that trick pulled many times before. He could have kept us younger guys, had he wanted to, and instead asked a couple of the older guys to consider retiring a little earlier than they'd planned. But he didn't.

My boss's countenance fell upon hearing my words.

He opened his mouth as if to say something, but changed his mind. After a few awkward moments, all he could muster was, "You're right."

I picked up my papers, thanked him for having had the chance to work there, turned around, and left. As I walked away, I realized that I wasn't angry with my supervisor. It wasn't his fault. I was the one who put myself in that situation. I was the one willing to work for a company that every year took jobs away from its people. Nothing comes with guarantees. I didn't regret the experience of having worked there, short-lived as it was. I managed to get my foot in the door, whereas some people are afraid to ever knock on the door.

> When you are inspired and a great idea comes, do not second guess, doubt, or delay. Just run with it. You can't lose.
>
> *Isaiah Fleurimond*

The layoff propelled me to set into motion the idea of creating my own destiny. I made a decision: at some point in time, I would be working for myself. I didn't know how I'd do it, or how long it would take, but I knew that one day, I'd be my own boss. No more layoffs for me.

Two years later, I learned that my former supervisor was laid off. As far as I know, he never worked again.

"Get Out Of My Yard, Nigger!"

The day I lost my job at the aerospace firm, I climbed into my car and drove to the utility company. I filled out an application, and then I called back every single day. Three weeks later, I had a new job. I became a meter reader for the public utility company. Once again, determination played a big role.

Like the postman, I was out every day, rain or shine, walking from house to house reading electric meters. I took my job seriously and did it well, breaking records as the company's fastest person to read meters with accuracy. In an eight-hour shift, I read anywhere from four hundred to one thousand meters, depending on how far apart the houses were spaced and how many obstacles I encountered. If it rained, I just kept on walking my route. If there was lightning, though, I had to wait in my car until the storm passed.

> Good men should not shrink from hardships and difficulties, nor complain against fate; they should take in good part whatever happens, and should turn it to good. Not what you endure, but how you endure, is important.
>
> *Seneca The Younger*

In most of the neighborhoods on my routes, there weren't many African Americans living there. I can't tell you how many times people called the police on me, thinking I was breaking into homes. Many times people cursed me out... until they realized I was just the meter guy doing my job. They even let their dogs out on me. I had a number of frightening encounters with big, mean dogs. Maybe it was the Lord's way of letting me know what my sister had felt when we were little kids and my brother and I would leave her alone with our growling dog!

At one particular house, the meter was hard to access, because it was located well behind the fence. As I leaned over, trying to read it, I noticed the owner of the house looking at me through his sliding glass door. Without hesitating, he let out his pit bull. The angry little beast charged at me, practically foaming at the mouth, and jumped up to take a bite as I leaned over the fence. I pulled back just in time. I looked up at the man and yelled, "I'm with the public utility company. I'm here to read your meter. Can you please get your dog?"

For a moment he stared, and then he turned his back on me and walked away. Meanwhile Fido continued to jump up and snarl viciously. Whenever I tried to get a reading there he was, ready to take a chunk out of me. I yelled at the man several more times (I could see him watching me through a window), asking him to put his dog back inside. Finally, I gave up. No way could I get a reading. I pressed the "Can't Read" button on my hand-held reader. This sent a signal back to the home office indicating that something was blocking this resident's meter. Which meant that the guy was going to get a well-deserved sky-high "estimated usage" bill the next time around.

As I walked to the next house, the man came running after me. "Did you read my meter?" he asked.

> You can only hope to find a lasting solution to a conflict if you have learned to see the other person objectively, but, at the same time, to experience his difficulties subjectively.
>
> *Dag Hammarskjold*

"How could I with your dog trying to bite my face off? I asked you to take your dog inside, and you didn't. You turned your back on me. I asked you several more times, and you didn't respond. Now if you'll excuse me, I've got a job to do." I don't know who was angrier at that moment, him or his pit bull.

The next month, I had no problem whatsoever reading his meter. As soon as he saw me, he called his dog inside and let me do my job.

The utility company did its best to keep its meter readers safe. Most of the time, we had advance warning regarding dogs, horses, and other potential dangers at specific addresses. We were also given special instructions when needed. We accessed all of this information through our handheld readers. At one particular property located in a lovely wooded area, the instructions for me were, "Horse present—make sure to close the gate." Okay, no problem.

I watched the horse out of the corner of my eye as I read the meter. He started to walk towards me. I got the reading and turned to look at him directly. He kept his eyes on me. I began to walk away, continuing with my route, when suddenly, he charged! Propelled by fear, I turned into track star Jesse Owens and took off as fast as my legs would move. The horse was right behind me. I had a hundred feet to go... I was running like Forest Gump. By some small miracle I outran that horse. I never looked back, and I never went back. To this day I don't know if I closed the gate.

> To act is to be committed, and to be committed is to be in danger.
>
> *James Baldwin*

I suspected nothing at another address. My handheld gave me no advance warning, so I confidently walked to the back of the house, passed through a gate, and made a couple of left turns before finding the meter on the wall. To my right, in the back of the garage, was an open side door. Unbeknownst to me, a white pit bull was sleeping inside. He walked to the door, groggy with sleep, and for just a moment I thought everything was going to be alright.

I was quite wrong. A mad look appeared across his face, and he charged full speed ahead. He jumped on my foot and started to tear my shoe. I managed to kick him off. He charged right back. This time I was ready. He froze in midair, stunned by the stream of pepper spray I directed his way. Yelping in pain, he took off running, and I got out of there as fast as I could.

At another house, a cute little Caucasian kid, about four years old, was playing out front with his baby sister. As I walked across his yard to the meter at the side of his house, he looked up at me with his big blue eyes and screamed, "Get out of my yard, nigger!"

> "Sticks and stones may break my bones but words will never hurt me," is one of the greatest deceptions ever, because words can kill you.
>
> *Isaiah Fleurimond*

Now I knew this little guy didn't know what he was saying. He wasn't even in school yet. I figured he must have heard it on television or from a neighbor or something. I decided to knock on the door and, very politely, explain to his Momma that he'd just said something she probably wouldn't want him to say.

"Ma'am, I'm sorry to bother you, but I felt you'd want to know what your little boy just said to me. I know you're raising him right, and you wouldn't approve of him calling me a nigger. He probably picked it up somewhere. I just felt I needed to let you know."

"I am so sorry!" she apologized. "I can't believe he'd say that. Timmy, come here!"

Her son dutifully walked over. She slapped his bottom. "I don't want you to say that again, you hear me? You're done playing outside. Get in here!"

I continued with my route down the street, returning mere moments later across the street. I noticed that the little boy was already back outside, playing as if nothing had happened. Had he learned anything?

On To Bigger And Better Things

After a year of reading meters and putting up with weather extremes, mean dogs, and rude people, I decided it was time to move on. I put in my transfer request to go into corporate security. I was accepted. I became facility operator, which involved monitoring all of the utility company's facilities from Key West to Tallahassee. The position came with tremendous responsibility. Working at the corporate office, I got to know the CEO and the president very well. To my delight, both of them were very nice, really cool guys.

> Ambition is the fuel of achievement
> *Joseph Epstein*

I had to pinch myself to make sure I wasn't dreaming. How does a kid who barely graduated high school with a 2.0 GPA get to where I was, monitoring major facilities throughout the state from a multimillion-dollar company's corporate headquarters? The only thing I could figure was this: With persistence, you can get *anywhere* in life.

Success Story

Héctor Ruiz

As CEO of computer chip manufacturer Advanced Micro Devices (AMD) since 2002, Héctor de Jesús Ruiz focuses not only on making a profit but also on making a difference. He's led his company on a number of corporate responsibility initiatives to help communities and protect the environment. AMD is a founding member of the One Laptop Per Child initiative, which aims to provide schoolchildren around the world, particularly in developing nations, with durable, sturdy, practical, and highly economical laptop computers to help with their education and advancement. It's no surprise that Héctor embraced this venture enthusiastically. After all, he knows firsthand what a difference an educational opportunity can make in one's life.

He was born in a border town in Mexico where his father managed livestock and his mother worked as a secretary. Héctor shined shoes in the town square, and he hoped to one day become an auto mechanic. After a missionary from the U.S. met Héctor and his family and was impressed by this bright young man, she persuaded the family to allow him to attend school in Texas. They agreed, and every day he walked across the border forty-five minutes to school, then forty-five minutes back home. Only three years after learning English, Héctor graduated from the American high school as school valedictorian. From there he went on to the University of Texas in Austin where he received engineering degrees. Later, he earned his Ph.D. in quantum electronics at Rice University. Before becoming CEO of AMD, he worked at Texas Instruments and Motorola.

He's reached great heights, but he's never forgotten his humble beginnings. Héctor has gone back to his birthplace to help his town, financially assisting the schools there. He is committed to empowering the children of his hometown as well as the children of the world through his global initiatives. In addition to working on the One Child Per Laptop program, Héctor launched his company's 50x15 initiative. Its goal is to bring affordable Internet access to at least 50% of the world's population by the year 2015. Knowing what a difference education has made in his life, this CEO is committed to using technology to promote and advance education around the world. He shows us that reaching the top is only half of the dream. The rest of the dream is to turn around, extend a hand, and help others reach new heights.

CHAPTER 7
Barber School Break

Train your head and hands to do, your head and heart to dare.

*Joseph Seamon Cotter,
poet, educator, playwright*

Barber School Break

I had the best supervisor in the world. Richard treated me and everyone in his group with nothing but respect. I knew his family, as he had Kim and me over to his house many times for dinners and social gatherings. Not only did he treat others right, he also treated himself right, since he neither drank nor smoked. He was a fine human being.

Unfortunately, he wasn't my supervisor for long. A new guy came aboard; I'll call him "Joe." He'd been laid off from his department and somehow managed to join ours. Richard took good care of him, the way he took care of all of us. He treated Joe right, watching out for him. But Joe didn't know how to reciprocate in kind. All he knew how to do was stab people in the back. He was a very cutthroat person.

> Do to others as you would have them do to you.
>
> *Luke* 6:31, NIV

Whenever some of the other department heads and supervisors went outside to smoke, Joe was right there with them, puffing on his cigarette and forming secret alliances. It seemed like he was out there every ten minutes. When the next layoffs hit, everyone in our department was safe... except for Richard. Joe had found a way to get rid of him *and* take over his job.

I'll never forget that day. Richard was devastated. He was practically in tears. So were the rest of us. We didn't want to see him go. But we weren't the decision makers. Joe, a smug smile of victory plastered across his face, strutted into Richard's barely vacated office, sat down, put his feet up on the desk, called his wife, and said, "Yeah, I got it." Disgraceful.

Tapping Into My Natural Talent

From the start it was clear Joe didn't like me. I don't know if it's because I was the only black guy in the department, or if our personalities simply clashed, but it wasn't long before he started poking shots at me. I evaded him as much as possible and continued doing my job monitoring multiple company facilities. My team and I were responsible for security in more than fifty sites. We monitored, investigated, and resolved any suspicious activity. Whenever high-level executives were flown in by helicopter from other plants, we escorted these VIPS into our headquarter buildings. I was responsible for keeping all of the facilities secure and keeping top-level people, especially the CEO, safe at all times. Every day was different and interesting. I loved my job.

> Talent is never enough; you have to have the love and heart for what you do.

At the same time, I decided to go to barber school. It was a decision I'd been putting off for a long time. I knew I had the talent; it's just something I was born with. Whenever I picked up clippers, every haircut turned out nice. Both my mother and Kim were cosmetologists, and both of them made good money. I could be making good money, too. All I needed was the certification. So I finally took the leap and enrolled in Palm Beach Beauty & Barber School.

By day I worked for the electric company from seven in the morning to 3:30 p.m., and at night I went to barber school from six to nine. Before long, Joe discovered I was going to night school, and he decided to make life difficult for me.

"Aldric," he said, "I need to make a couple of changes here. I'm moving you to the later shift. Starting next week you'll work from three in the afternoon to midnight. Can you do that?" He watched me closely for a reaction.

I took a deep breath and stayed calm. "No problem," I replied with a smile. He looked disappointed.

> Men rise from one ambition to another: First they seek to secure themselves against attack and then attack others.
>
> *Machiavelli*

I simply rearranged my day to make it work. At barber school, I switched over to daytime hours. I went to school from eight a.m. to two p.m., starting my shift with the utility company at three in the afternoon. In some ways it was better. The switch gave me more hours in school, which meant I was moving through the program faster, and I'd have my barber's license sooner.

Joe didn't like seeing me come in to work happy and upbeat. Before long, he switched me over again, assigning me to the midnight shift. He was determined to get rid of me, just like he got rid of Richard. But I was determined, too. I did everything in my power to keep my job and continue with school.

My weekly schedule became a marathon. I worked at company headquarters from 11:30 p.m. to seven in the morning. Then I got to barber school by eight and attended classes from nine a.m. to six p.m. I went home, slept for three hours, and headed back to work. It was crazy, but I stuck with it.

Joe thought he was hurting me, but in reality, he ended up helping me. Like the old saying goes, the devil made it for bad, but God turned it for good. Every time Joe tried to slow me down, I didn't miss a beat. I was just as sharp as he was. I used every one of his moves to my advantage in our little chess game. In the end, with God's help, I finished barber school faster than I'd originally planned. Instead of taking me eighteen months, it took me only twelve months to complete the program.

My Janitorial Stint

I did leave the company, though. Having Joe for a supervisor was the pits. I reached the point where I just didn't want to have to report to him any longer. It was degrading, and I didn't want his garbage in my life anymore. I left the utility company before completing barber school, and I vowed to *never* work in the corporate world again. I was tired of the games people played. Corporate America is not "user friendly," I found out. Only shareholders count for something; employees are completely dispensable.

> Ambition never is in a great hurry than I; it merely keeps pace with circumstances and with my general way of thinking.
>
> *Napoleon*

I had to find a way to pay for school, which I wasn't about to quit. It cost $250 a month to attend. So I came up with an idea. "Would it be possible for me to clean the school on Mondays in exchange for tuition?" I asked the staff. Monday was the school's day off. "I'll do the toilets, windows, mopping, and vacuuming. I'll get everything cleaned up nicely before classes start on Tuesday." After clearing it with the supervisor, they gave me the green light.

Every Monday, I went in and did my janitorial work

diligently. Often Kim came along and helped me out. What I earned as a janitor went straight to my tuition. In this manner I stayed in school, and I got my barber's license, which enabled me to start working for myself the way I'd dreamed about. No more nasty supervisors. No more layoff worries. No more getting jerked around from one shift to another. I could finally be my own boss.

By the way, Kim was no longer my girlfriend. Kim had become my wife.

A Wedding To Remember

We'd been married a year by the time I became a barber. I was twenty-four and working for the utility company when I married my high school sweetheart. It truly was a wedding to remember. We had talked about having a nice traditional church wedding, but deep down both of us wanted to do something different, something that would really stand out and have people talking for years. So we chose to get married on a beautiful, old-fashioned paddleboat. Kim and I exchanged our vows before family and friends while the picturesque boat was docked. Then it sailed from beautiful Singer Island, and we spent the next three hours eating and celebrating aboard, cruising across Florida's aquamarine waters.

> Life without commitment is not worth living.
> *Abraham Joshua Heschel*

I'm proud that we tried to do everything right. I'm

not talking just about our beautiful wedding. I mean we didn't live together before we got married. We wanted to do things the right way and have the Lord's blessing upon our marriage. Kim and I got to know each other first, established a deep friendship, and even made and saved enough money so we'd be okay financially as we began our lives together. We made sure that as husband and wife, each of us always put the other person first. I consulted with Kim before making any major decision. When I decided to go to barber school, I had my wife's blessing. And when I decided to leave the utility company, she agreed that it was the right thing to do.

Of course, our relatives, especially our moms, are very important to us, but as newlyweds we made sure to establish that we'd make our *own* decisions as a married couple and not have family make our decisions for us. It's perfectly fine to go to our parents and ask for advice, but we'd never allow our in-laws to get involved in our personal affairs. This has worked well for us.

> A problem is defined and isolated; information is gathered; alternatives are set forth; an end is established; means are created to achieve that end; a choice is made.
>
> *James MacGregor*

My wife and I are the youngest children of our respective families. When she began working as a cosmetologist, and later I started working as a barber, we became the first in our families to be self-employed. We were also the first of all the siblings to build a home from the ground up. I'm so proud of what Kim and I have accomplished together.

I firmly believe that with enough fortitude, dedication, and resolve, anybody can overcome other people's criticism to forge his or her own path and accomplish wonderful things. I also firmly believe that when you have the right person by your side as your partner in life, together you can do just about anything! Each day I thank God for my very special gal, who keeps inspiring me every step of the way.

Success Story

Hal Taussig, Christian Businessman & Philanthropist

Some people measure success by how much money they make. Others measure success by how much money they give away and how many people they help. That's how Hal Taussig defines success. He lives his passion of connecting cultures through his travel company, Untours, which he founded with his wife Norma. He treats his staff with care and dignity; they are paid above-average salaries and they get to spend two weeks in Europe each year. But most admirable is the fact that Hal has no desire to be a rich man. He gives almost all of his company's profits to his foundation, which strives to create jobs, build affordable housing, and promote fair trade.

His generosity has not gone unnoticed. The late John F. Kennedy, Jr. and Paul Newman presented Hal and Norma with an award in 1999 recognizing Untours as the "Most Generous Company in America." Hal and his wife live modestly. The octogenarian doesn't even own a car, and he rides to work on a bicycle. He's given millions of dollars away to help low-income earners get off welfare, secure jobs, start their own thriving businesses, and improve their lives in many ways. Hal's generosity shows that you can be perfectly happy living your passion, living modestly, and giving from your heart to help others flourish.

CHAPTER 8
Finding My Way

The road of life twists and turns and no two directions are ever the same.

Yet our lessons come from the journey, not the destination.

*Don Williams,
Jr., novelist, poet*

Finding My Way

The Bible says that you can minister wherever you're at. I can attest to that. I minister from my barber's chair. In essence, I am a barbershop counselor, simply by being a good listener and allowing people to express their pain, their joys, their most heartfelt thoughts, and then sharing with them how the Lord makes a difference in my life. I've seen huge, three hundred pound guys come to Christ in this chair, and afterwards they're so moved they cry like a baby. People of all ages, from young kids all the way up to the elderly have received Jesus Christ while sitting in this very chair where I give haircuts. God's doing the work here, not me. I feel privileged to be able to witness so many spiritual transformations.

> You have to trust your inner knowing. If you have a clear mind and an open heart, you won't have to search for direction. Direction will come to you.
>
> *Phil Jackson*

But I'm getting ahead of myself here. Let me go back and explain how it all started and how my "barbershop ministry" came to be... The seeds were planted when I was in barber school. While still a student, I began working and practicing at the same salon where my mom and wife worked. Mom had her own chair, Kim had hers, and I had mine, all of us working as independent contractors. Little by little I built up my clientele, and by the time I finished school and got my license at the age of twenty-five, I had a well-established customer base that included pro athletes, celebrities, and successful business people. What do you suppose baseball's Deion Sanders and Scarborough Green, basketball's Horace Grant, and football's Jimmy Spencer have in common, other than being successful sports figures? That's right; they've all received haircuts from me.

Working many hours week after week, it wasn't long before I became a "Master Barber." Through word of mouth my clientele continued to grow. I quickly gained a reputation as the barber who could do *any* cut and make it stylish. After all those years of searching for my place in the world, of encountering obstacles in school and the military, of working for others, I finally felt like a success in business for myself. Yes, I worked hard, but I had a ball. I can't think of any other profession where your friends, family, and neighbors can come over, talk with you all day long, *and* you get paid for it!

> Recall the face of the poorest and the most helpless man whom you may have seen and ask yourself, if the step you contemplate is going to be of any use to him. Will he be able to gain anything by it? Will it restore him to a control over his own life and destiny?
>
> *Mohandas Gandhi*

Whenever a client made himself comfortable in my barber chair and took the weight off his feet and off his shoulders for a moment, he'd invariably open up about his life. I always made sure to listen attentively while I cut his hair. A barbershop or beauty salon, I quickly discovered, is a community of people gathered *not* to gossip (as stereotypes like to insinuate) but to find information that'll better themselves and perhaps serve someone close to them. Part of my job became trying to help them put solutions to their problems. My main job, though, other than cutting hair, was to *listen*. I always like to say that God gave us one mouth and two ears so we can listen twice as much as we speak.

Just like I did in high school when I wanted to converse with my teachers, I paid attention to current events so I could have meaningful conversations with my clients. I tried to stay on top of events both in my community and in the world. When someone came in feeling down and blue, I'd start talking about an interesting news story to distract them. See, people come in not just to get beautified but also to get their spirit uplifted. In our modern-day society, all of us are so consumed by our own little worlds and dramas that we just don't make the time to talk with people as we go about our everyday business.

Think about the grocery store. Some of the elderly people there who perhaps haven't talked to another soul all week are dying to connect with someone through a smile, a bright hello, or a few friendly words. And what do we do? We brush right past them, grab the groceries we need, and hurry to the checkout stand without even making eye contact. What people crave most is real conversation with real people. That's exactly what they get at our barber shop.

> Knowledge is organized and accessible information; wisdom is knowledge used effectively in the service of worthy ends.
>
> *Anonymous*

Whenever I learned something valuable from one client, I always made it a point to share it with another who could benefit from that piece of information. I'm not talking about spilling the beans or revealing private matters. I never betrayed anyone's trust. I was merely an "information hub." If someone needed some financial advice, for example, I shared with him something useful I'd learned earlier from a businessman whose hair I'd cut. That's the beauty of the barbershop. With your haircut you get a free dose of practical *and* inspirational advice.

I've enjoyed tremendous success and satisfaction as a

barber, but I didn't reach this level of success by myself. God directed my path every step of the way, and He gave me a beautiful, supportive wife to encourage me forward. After sixteen years, Kim and I still cut hair side by side at the salon, which we now own. People often ask me how we can work together and live together and still get along as well as we do. I tell them that it's God's work. When you love what you do, love the person you're with, and love the Lord, life is good.

It was risky for me to leave the utility company to start off on my own. But that's how a person reaches his or her success—by trying, struggling, learning something from the experience, and trying again. We have to take certain risks to reach our success. We have to be willing to try. That's one of the secrets to success.

Another secret is this: You have to be willing to help others along the way. In business, *your* name doesn't always have to come first. Let others' names be at the forefront sometimes. Give the folks you're working with the recognition and appreciation they deserve, and the job will get done just fine.

Trying Something New

With my confidence built up as a successful barber, I branched out into a new venture. I decided I wanted to become a realtor, for several reasons. First, talking to realtors who came to my shop motivated me to learn everything I could about realty. I was intrigued; could I *really* buy real estate with no money down? Or maybe I could purchase properties using the commission I'd be making as a realtor. In any case, with the wealth of information

I'd learn as a realtor, surely I'd be able to share valuable tips with my loyal barbershop clients and help them out.

> Do not seek for information of which you cannot make use.
>
> *Anna C. Brackett*

Then there was the challenging aspect of trying something different and unfamiliar. I've never shied away from a new challenge. Realty was something completely new to me, and I got a certain thrill thinking about putting myself through this newest challenge. As always, there were the doomsayers telling me that I couldn't do it, that it was way too hard, and that it was well beyond my reach. I wasn't about to let them be right. I made it a point to prove them wrong and prove to myself that I *could* do it.

But just as in high school and in the military, exams and I didn't get along. I went to class and felt I had learned everything satisfactorily, but I failed the real estate test by just two points. Déjà vu. I didn't give up, though. I had no intention of letting those folks who claimed I couldn't do it rub it in with a chorus of *I told you so*. I hadn't spent all that time attending class and studying just to be defeated. I registered to take that test again. It was scheduled for a Monday morning; Sunday my wife and I came home from church, and I went straight upstairs to my office.

"Kim, I'm going to be studying up here until tomorrow."

> Someone's negative comment about you does not have to be your reality.
>
> *Anonymous*

"Alright, Aldric, just let me know if you need anything."

I began studying at two in the afternoon and kept going nonstop until nine that evening. I took a short break and grabbed a bite to eat, then went right back to studying. Sometime after three in the morning I took a power nap, waking up at 4:00 AM. I hit the books again, studying until it was time for me to drive out and take that test.

This time I had a really good feeling. When the exam was over, I knew I'd passed. The woman in charge confirmed what I already knew, and I had my realtor's license. I made it! I joined the team at American Dream Realty. Serious about becoming a top realtor, I challenged myself by taking extra courses, including those designed for mortgage brokers, in order to learn every angle of the business.

My favorite part of the job was talking with clients and showing them around. I could always talk people into taking a look at a home on the market. That was the easy part. What I *couldn't* do was talk them into buying a home that I'd never purchase for my wife and me. If the property was too close to a major road, or right next to high voltage power lines, or the roof leaked, or it was flawed in any way, I didn't have the heart to close the deal. I talked the buyer out of the purchase. That made me a very poor realtor. But I just couldn't do it. I take seriously Jesus' directive to love your neighbor as yourself. I couldn't sell my neighbor a house I wouldn't live in.

My days as a realtor were short-lived. I did this for about six months before realizing it just wasn't my cup of tea. But hey, I gave it a shot, and I learned a great deal in the process and built up more leadership skills. None of what I learned went to waste. The knowledge I gained as a realtor helped me to better understand that market. It gave me the tools I needed to go out and buy real estate on my own. It also enabled me to give my barbershop clients sound advice when they wanted to purchase a house. Nothing learned is ever in vain. Any knowledge we gain can help us and those around us, in some way.

Receiving Christ

In the world's eyes I was a very successful man. I had a beautiful home, several cars, my own business, a good income, and nice clothes—stuff that would make some folks green with envy. But despite everything I had achieved and acquired, I'd begun to feel an emptiness inside. It was so strange. Suddenly, I didn't *feel* successful anymore. I felt that I was missing something important, something big, because despite all that I had attained, despite my wonderful marriage and all the fabulous people in my life, I wasn't very happy on the inside. Each day I began to grow more frustrated with myself, more pessimistic about the world I lived in. I couldn't quite put my finger on it, but I just felt like there had to be more to life and success than this.

Finding My Way

> The purpose of life is undoubtedly to know oneself. We cannot do it unless we learn to identify ourselves with all that lives. The sum total of that life is God. Hence the necessity of realizing God living within every one of us.
>
> *Mohandas K. Gandhi*

I drove to work one Saturday morning in my red Ford Splash pickup truck listening to Dr. Adrian Rogers, a Baptist pastor, on WRMB 89.3 FM. His inspiring words always moved me. I'd grown up in the Baptist faith, and I'd gone to church my whole life. I always enjoyed the church experience, especially the music, but nothing had ever propelled me to act like Dr. Rogers' words did that morning. He ended his message to his listeners with these powerful words, "Do you want to receive Christ as your savior? You may think you're successful in the world's eyes, but you're not successful in God's eyes unless you receive His Son."

Boy, was he talking to me! His message came straight at me like a flaming arrow of light. Something stirred in my heart and deep within my soul. I didn't want to feel dead inside anymore. It was time. With tears in my eyes and conviction in my heart, I prayed. I asked God to take away that awful feeling that had started to consume me and to fill me with His love. Right then and there, in the truck during my Saturday morning commute, I asked Jesus Christ to come into my heart.

It was the moment that changed everything. On the surface, nothing had changed, but on the inside, *everything* had changed. I was a new creation. As soon as I got to a phone I called Kim and told her what just happened. She was so moved. For the next two weeks, I was on a natural high. That emptiness I had been living with faded away, and in its place came a feeling of peace coupled with a new resolve, a new purpose. I devoted myself to serving God. I shifted from focusing on myself to focusing on empowering others.

Success Story

Wally Amos, Entrepreneur, Actor, & Writer

After his mother and father divorced, then twelve-year-old Wallace "Wally" Amos, Jr. moved from Florida to New York to live with his aunt, who became his parental figure and was an exceptional role model for him. She was the first person ever to bake him chocolate chip cookies; her recipes inspired his own later in life. It would be a while before he became an entrepreneur, though. First he served in the Air Force, worked at Saks Fifth Avenue, and became a talent agent for the William Morris Agency in New York, the firm's first African-American agent.

He developed an ingenious way to attract and thank talent—he baked cookies for them. Wally represented a number of rising stars (now superstars), including Diana Ross, Simon & Garfunkel, and the Temptations. After several years with William Morris, he opened his own agency and relocated to Los Angeles.

At the age of thirty-eight, Wally shifted gears completely and opened his first Famous Amos cookie store on Hollywood's Sunset Boulevard, turning his weekend hobby into a fulltime venture. He borrowed $25,000 from friends to help make his dream a reality. Wally worked hard to make his business succeed, ever promoting his product through his positive, outgoing personality. He baked his own cookies, passed them out on the streets, and delivered them to friends. His approach worked. By his third year in business, Wally had added two more baking and manufacturing facilities as well as additional stores in California and his first store in Hawaii. He moved to Hawaii, where he continues to reside today.

He sold his company years ago, but he's never stopped living life to the fullest. Wally has authored eight books, launched a muffin company, become a literacy advocate, and served as the national spokesperson for Literacy Volunteers of America for twenty-three years. He and his wife started a foundation to promote reading aloud to children. He's traveled the world as an inspirational speaker, and he's appeared on several sitcoms and countless television interview spots and commercials. His many achievements have been recognized through awards and honors, including the Horatio Alger Award and the President's Award For Entrepreneurial Excellence.

Wally teaches us to seize the opportunities that come our way and to thoroughly enjoy the work we're doing. He once said, "There are people who convince themselves that they can't do anything with their lives because of what's happened to them—and they're right. They can't. But the reason is that they've told themselves they can't. They've said, 'I am a victim. Somebody did something to me that paralyzed me for life.' If you believe that, you'll never move forward."

CHAPTER 9
Playing Spiritual Catch-up

There are only two ways to live your life.
One is as though nothing is a miracle.
The other is as though everything is a miracle.

*Albert Einstein,
scientist, physicist*

Playing Spiritual Catch-up

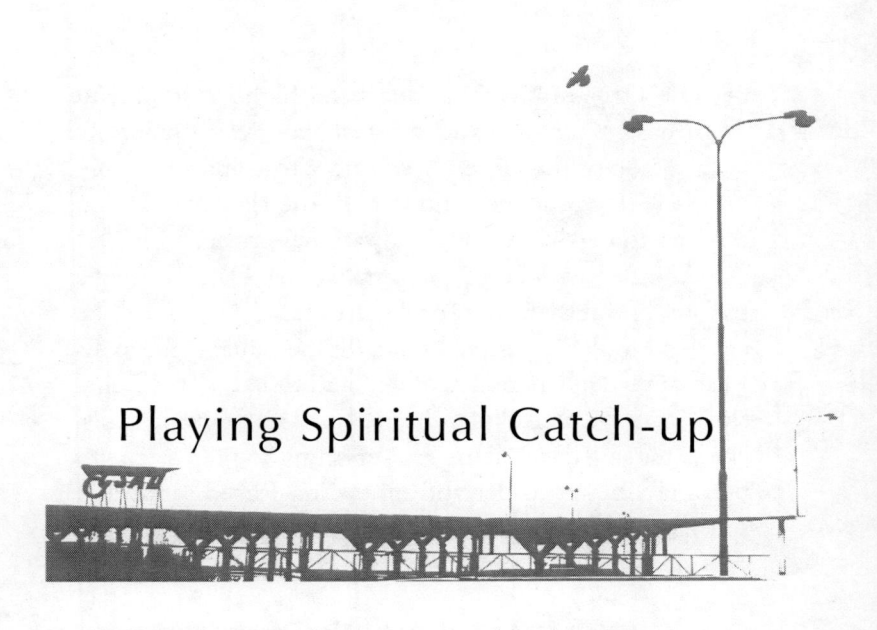

To best help others, I believe you have to be as fit and sharp as you can be in every sense—in your mind, in your spirit, in the way you communicate with others, and in how your words touch their hearts and stir their souls. When you work to improve yourself, expanding your knowledge base, skills, and abilities, you end up in a better position to encourage and assist your fellow man. With this in mind, I continued with my personal training. I joined Toastmasters International, known around the world as the organization that teaches you how to get up in front of an audience and speak confidently, without fainting or hyperventilating, and in an engaging style.

Now, I've never had a problem talking to people. I don't get nervous, and I do know how to lift others up. But Toastmasters helped me to take these skills to the next level and speak more eloquently. They helped me become a true motivational speaker. I highly recommend Toastmasters for all of you, whatever your vocation or life path may be. They'll teach you how to stand up before others with confidence and choose the right words and delivery to maximize your inspirational impact.

Another wonderful program is the Dale Carnegie training. I did that, too, and I can't praise it enough. The courses I took through them taught me valuable life skills I can apply anywhere. I acquired additional motivational skills, management skills, interpersonal relationship skills, character skills, you name it, everything to prepare me to become a better leader and motivator. I even received a special recognition pin for my speaking abilities and my capacity to relate positively to others.

> Learn in order to teach and to practice.
>
> *Talmud*

I recommend that each of you take some form of Dale Carnegie training. You'll gain practical, essential leadership skills. You'll grow by leaps and bounds in many areas of self-improvement, and you'll learn how to build others' self-worth, too. After I started getting into the Word more, I realized that both of these programs, Dale Carnegie and Toastmasters, essentially base their teachings and material on what Christ says in the Bible. That's why these programs work so well and are so popular around the world—they're based on universal truths.

A Higher Calling

After receiving Christ, I felt moved to do more with my life. I felt I was being called into the ministry. Although I'd gone to church ever since I could remember, I suddenly had a deep desire to learn everything about Jesus Christ—who he was and what, exactly, he did, said, and taught during his earthly ministry. I wanted to know how I could apply his teachings more completely in my life as well as the history of the Bible and what instructions it has for me. I knew bits and pieces, but I hungered for the entire big picture. I began to play "spiritual catch-up."

My first step was to enroll in a Christian school, South Florida Bible College, with the intent of learning everything I could about the Bible and ultimately becoming pastor of a church. I loved reading the Bible. Doing so opened up so many truths for me. I relished this journey of spiritual discovery. I had a tremendous desire to share what I was learning with others, to make a difference in their lives, so soon I started a program called Men On A Mission. It met—where else? At the barbershop.

It was basically a support group for at-risk kids. I provided for them a safe environment to air their grievances, and I gave them tools to help them move forward with their lives. Every Monday night they met at the barbershop and talked about whatever was plaguing them, whether it be drugs, alcohol, peer pressure, problems at school, or issues with parents. Half my job was to listen to them ... I mean *really* listen, because too often kids are the most alienated people in the world. I'm sure you've heard the expression, "Children should be seen and not heard." This is so wrong! Kids *need* to be heard.

> Youth is the seed time of good habits, as well in nations as in individuals.
>
> *Thomas Paine*

They've got feelings, ideas, dreams, hopes, and fears: We adults must do a better job of encouraging them to express these. Often what happens in our society is that we push kids aside as if they're nobody, and we keep doing this until they're twelve or thirteen… and then it's too late. Kids have a voice. They have an opinion, and they long to be heard and taken seriously.

So each Monday night I let these young men talk, and I listened carefully, never putting them down or belittling what they had to say. Then, after they got everything off their chests, we worked on solutions. Together we sought ways for them to say no to drugs and negative peer pressure, get along better with parents and teachers, and find a positive direction for themselves. We prayed together, and we studied the Bible together. I am very proud of this ministry. I know these kids' parents were very thankful for it as well.

I continued to attend Bible college for almost a year when I suddenly received a message from above. "You need no man to teach you what the Holy Spirit teaches you," was the thought that the Spirit impressed upon me. I pondered what this could mean. I shared it with my wife, and after thinking and talking about it we both realized that the Holy Spirit was telling me that Bible school wasn't exactly where I needed to be at that point in my life. I had thought that I was to become a minister at a church, but I came to realize that this wasn't what God had in mind for me. God intended for me to minister out in the world, the way I'd been doing in the barbershop with my clients and with the Monday evening support group. I left Bible college, and I kept reading and studying the Bible on my own.

Back To School

I continued working at the barbershop and doing my ministry there. Whenever I gave a haircut, I also spoke of Christ. This is how it came to be that so many people received Jesus Christ while sitting in my barber's chair. Parents asked me to talk to their sons who had stopped listening to them and started off in the wrong direction. People who were hurting inside for all kinds of reasons came in, sometimes for a haircut and other times just to talk and hear the good news of Jesus Christ. Over the years I've had so many people tell me that they feel so much peace in this barber's chair. I know it's not me—it's the Lord's presence that they feel, bringing them love and healing.

> Find your purpose, study your purpose, live your purpose and then live out your purpose.

One Saturday morning I was standing at the barbershop, cutting someone's hair, when the Holy Spirit caught me by surprise and pierced me at my side. I almost said "ouch" out loud! But I remained silent and listened. I knew that when the Holy Spirit was getting my attention, I had better keep quiet and find out what he was trying to tell me.

The message was simple: *Go to school.*

Before I could complain and object that I'd already gone to school, that I had attended Bible college for nearly a year before being informed that I didn't need to go there anymore, I received a second spiritual clue. I was told that this time I was to study at Palm Beach Atlantic University. A big, intimidating university for somebody who'd graduated from high school with just a 2.0 GPA. I didn't even know if I'd be accepted.

But the message came clearly, so I knew I had to at least go to the campus and test the waters. I spoke with a very nice woman at the admissions office who encouraged me to apply. Nervous as I could be, I filled out the paperwork and took a writing test. Miraculously, they accepted me!

Palm Beach Atlantic is a Christian university that focuses on learning, leadership, and service and offers both undergraduate and graduate programs. Even though I was terrified going in, once I started taking classes I truly felt the presence of God. A sense of peace came over me I realized that with the help of God, I *could* do it. I chose to major in ministry, a comprehensive program that blends biblical, theological, historical, and practical studies. I absolutely loved it, so much so that I didn't even mind having a hectic schedule again.

By day I worked, and from six to ten in the evening I attended classes. By the time I got home, Kim was asleep, so I'd kiss her and then head downstairs to study until three or four in the morning. The amazing thing was that I wasn't even tired. I was so pumped up by the program, so excited by everything I was learning—theology, spiritual formation, Old Testament, New Testament, church in history, church in society, evangelism. I was completely enthralled.

No Worries

Academically, everything was going smoothly. The one aspect I worried about, though, was money. I received some financial aid in the form of grants, but in the back of my mind I kept asking myself, "How am I going to pay for this?"

> We are, perhaps, uniquely among the earth's creatures, the worrying animal. We worry away our lives, fearing the future, discontent with the present, unable to take in the idea of dying, unable to sit still.
>
> *Lewis Thomas*

One night, I had a dream. In my dream, I was troubled, wondering where the money was going to come from to pay for school. I was so consumed by this worry that I turned to God. "Lord," I asked, "where is this money coming from?" While I waited for an answer, I stared at a collection of books sitting high on a bookshelf. As long as I focused on the books, a stream of water filled with live fish fell off the bookshelf onto the top of my head! (What can I say, it was a dream.) I began to wonder where all of the water and fish were coming from. Curious, I scaled the bookshelf and peered over the top, looking for the source. But when I did this, the water stopped flowing and the live fish stopped falling. Instead, I saw dead fish.

I woke up and pondered this dream, thinking how bizarre and vivid it was. As I thought about it, trying to make sense of it, God spoke to my spirit, saying, "If you worry about where the money's coming from, it'll stop coming." The flow would cease. I got the hint. From then on, I worried about it no more.

College Graduate

With nothing to distract or worry me any longer, I poured myself into my studies. I'm not sure how I did it, but I never missed any homework, I always got A's on my assignments, and I managed to complete all my projects. I did everything I needed to do to successfully complete the coursework. I felt as though the Holy Spirit was directing me, instructing me what to do, how to do it, and when to do it. I can't take credit for any of that.

> The whole secret of a successful life is to find out what it is one's destiny to do, and then do it.
>
> *Henry Ford*

I enjoyed my classes so much that I completed the four-year program in just three and a half years. I graduated from Palm Beach Atlantic University with a Bachelor's in Ministry. And something else ... I graduated with a 3.8 GPA. If a kid who couldn't read, was labeled a slow learner, and barely made it out of high school with a 2.0 GPA can go on to get a bachelor's degree from a university with a 3.8 GPA then nothing's impossible! With hope, persistence, and God, anything is possible.

Success Story

Midori Goto, Concert Violinist

There is no doubt that she was born with a God-given gift for music. When Midori Goto was just seven years old, she gave her first public violin performance. She's fortunate enough to have a supportive mother who first recognized her talent and then dedicated herself to helping her daughter flourish as a violinist. Midori's mother moved with her from their native Japan to the U.S. where she could learn from some of the best musicians in the world. In turn, Midori has worked hard and reached impressive musical heights for someone so young.

She's toured the world as a performer and has enjoyed a remarkable career as a soloist with the New York Philharmonic Orchestra, Berlin Philharmonic, the Boston Symphony Orchestra, the London Symphony Orchestra, and many other leading orchestras. But like every good steward, she knows that life is not just about pushing yourself to succeed. It's also about helping others along the way.

When Midori was twenty years old, she started a nonprofit organization to fund music education, including workshops and concerts, in New York public schools. She often performs at schools and openly shares her love of music with children. Her organization sponsors an annual day-long children's music festival in New York. In addition, she has launched a nonprofit organization in Japan to support music education in her birth country. She also helps young musicians through musical outreach programs in other nations. Midori does not keep her gift to herself. She shares it freely with others as a performer, teacher, and mentor so that they, too, can be empowered by music.

CHAPTER 10
Getting Others Motivated

People often say that motivation doesn't last.

Well, neither does bathing—that's why we recommend it daily.

Zig Ziglar,
author, motivational speaker, salesperson

Getting Others Motivated

While I was still a student at Palm Beach Atlantic University, Kim felt it was time for us to have kids. I agreed. After enjoying seven wonderful years as husband and wife, we were ready for our family to grow. First our son was born, and shortly thereafter, our daughter came into the world, both of them bringing a whole new dimension of joy, meaning, and responsibility into our lives. Let me tell you, being a parent is nothing short of amazing! It completely changes your perspective. I'm thankful that I received Christ before my children were born, because as a father I need all the guidance I can get. And to me, there's no better source of solid guidance than Jesus Christ.

With the growth of our family came a steep increase in our health insurance premiums. Kim and I, being self-employed, were self-insured. When our son was born, our monthly premium went from $560 to $840. And when our daughter was born, the premium jumped up to $1,200 a month. In a short span of time, the cost of our insurance *doubled,* and we could no longer afford it. I had to get another job, one that offered health coverage, to take care of my family.

I asked myself, *Where should I go look for work?* I wanted to be where I could make a difference, and I needed a job that offered enough flexibility to continue studying at the university and working at the barber shop. After careful consideration, I decided to see if the school board had any openings for me.

> To the world you're just one person, but to that one person you are the world.
>
> *Anonymous*

Sure enough, they did. I got a job as a police aide at a local high school. It was perfect. As I patrolled the school grounds in my little golf cart, I had the opportunity to meet and speak with many students. I couldn't help but think of Mr. Perry, the school police officer who was my "dad away from home" during my middle school years. My goal was to inspire and motivate everyone I encountered, just as Mr. Perry had motivated me so many years ago. I talked to these high school students about character, about doing the right thing, and pretty soon more and more were coming to me seeking advice or just an uplifting word. I never talked down to them, and I always made sure to validate everybody. Before going to their guidance counselor or the dean or the assistant principal, a lot of the students came to talk to me.

There were times when work was slow, and I could do my own homework, and this intrigued the kids. "Mr. Marshall, you back in school?" they asked. They were curious about what I was studying, and this opened a dialogue about their future. Always I advised them to move into a field that they loved doing. "Don't worry about the money," I told them, just as God had told me in my dream. "The money will come along if you love what you're doing. When you wake up in the morning and have so much enthusiasm to embrace the day, even if you're not getting paid, you'll be profitable because you enjoy what you're doing."

I also encouraged them to study *now* and not wait until they were thirty-five, like me. I didn't try to hide or sugarcoat things. I shared how I didn't like school when I was younger, how I struggled and didn't reach out for help. I let them know that because of my past challenges, I was genuinely nervous about studying at the university. And I encouraged them to finish school and have their careers well established before they started a family. That way they'd be able to spend more time with their children. Some days I truly missed being with my kids. With my busy schedule I couldn't always spend as much time with my young children as I wanted to. Certainly we had family time, and I saw my kids every day, but I wish I had more opportunities to read them bedtime stories or have tickle fights or simply sit and listen to whatever was on their minds. Some days I couldn't enjoy these simple pleasures because I had to study for a test or work extra hours at the barbershop.

> Half of the world is on the wrong scent in the pursuit of happiness. They think it consists in having and getting, and in being served by others. It consists in giving and serving others.
>
> *Henry Drummond*

At my day job, the high school students and I talked about everything under the sun. It wasn't long before I experienced a tremendous shift in my attitude. My original incentive was to get insurance for my family, but almost immediately I found a new motivation for doing my job. I was excited about making a positive impact on the community at large. I truly felt then, as I feel today, that when you take the time to talk to young people, listen to them, and mentor them, you're benefiting the entire community.

The school principal kept me on my toes, and at the same time she was very supportive. She allowed me to study for a test and do my homework when I needed to, all the while maintaining high expectations of me. "You can do your work," she permitted, "just keep the kids under control." I did. She showed me a few effective ways to deal with teens, especially the ones who were acting out. I took my job seriously, zipping around in that golf cart rain or shine, making sure nobody left or came to the campus without proper authorization and doing everything in my power to keep everyone safe.

After I'd been there a few months the principal approached me. "Aldric, do you have sixty credits yet at the university?" she asked. I sure did.

"Good," she continued. "I want to create a new behavior intervention program. I see how you go over and beyond to try to help these kids. I feel you'd be a great behavior intervention teacher. And with your sixty college credits, you qualify. What do you think?"

> You must be respectable, if you will be respected.
> *Lord Chesterfield*

I jumped at the opportunity. In this new position, I was to take the so-called "bad kids" and help straighten them out. I had my own classroom, and many of the students who previously would have been sent home or to the vice principal for poor behavior now were sent to my classroom. Often teachers would come into my room and say, "Mr. Marshall, you need to get so-and-so and bring him to your class for one period and just talk to him." I became something of a counselor to these kids, even though that wasn't my official title. My approach was simple and effective: I gave these kids the respect they wanted, and in turn they gave me the respect that I as a teacher needed. Students were always saying "hi" to me in the hallways. They'd go out of their way just to come say hello.

Safe School Ambassadors

My job continued to grow and evolve. Soon I became coordinator of the Safe School Ambassadors program at our school. This program was launched in California and has spread throughout the country. It relies on the principles of "peer helping," where teens are trained in violence prevention techniques and positive youth development and then serve as ambassadors within their own social circles. Students always are first in line, knowing what goes on, seeing who is getting bullied and harassed, so it makes sense to empower them with communication and intervention skills. They can then speak up and stop the bullying without resorting to violence. They learn how to keep the peace, how to stay safe, and when to turn to an adult for help. It's a wonderful program that respects kids and gets them involved, helping them to be positive leaders and role models for their peers.

I was amazed at how many kids wanted to be in the program! I trained as many students as I could, and for all the others who didn't have the official title of ambassador but still wanted to be involved, I offered pointers and encouraged them to be involved. I explained that they already were ambassadors, even without the official title. I taught mediation skills to everyone who wanted to learn, and our campus truly became a safer, friendlier place.

> No matter how busy you are, you must take time to make the other person feel important.
>
> *Mary Kay Ash*

Thanks to the success on our campus, I was asked to speak at other schools and train people there to run the Safe School Ambassadors program. I enjoyed this immensely. I was also asked to become a liaison between our school and parents in order to help kids who either were failing or weren't meeting the school's expectations in some area. As a liaison, my job was to recommend strategies and programs to help each student on a case by case basis.

Why was I given more and more responsibility? I don't have a psychology or counseling degree, but I do have a heart for kids, and I'm sure the school's administrators saw that. They were willing to train me, and I was willing to learn everything in order to create a better, safer school environment and help *every* student succeed. I did not mind taking on more responsibility, not at all.

Roadmap to Life

Another one of my roles was to serve as a substitute teacher. Whenever I subbed, I did one of two things. Either I asked, "Who knows the most in this class?" Everybody would point to that person, whom I'd then ask to get up and teach the class. It got that person out of his or her shell and won him or her the respect of peers. Or instead, I used that time as an open "question and answer" session.

"You never have time to ask your teachers questions because of your schoolwork," I stated to the students, and they agreed. "So today is your chance. Today we're having 'open forum,' and you can ask anything you want. We'll talk about whatever's on your mind." They loved it. I got all kinds of questions, from goofy to really serious and thought-provoking. And I did my best to answer honestly and with integrity.

I also did my best to get every student to see that this period of their lives matters. This is the time for them to learn everything they can to help them in their future endeavors. Every one of us, regardless of our age, gets so distracted at times that we forget to focus on what really matters. I saw this in school over and over again. Students get so distracted by phone calls, text messaging, electronic gadgets, popular music, boyfriends, girlfriends, going to the movies, hanging out at the mall, playing video games, you name it, that they fail to sit down and think about what really matters to them.

> Mission starts with determining what you really care about and want to accomplish and committing yourself to it. You can always develop expertise. First, discover your preference.
>
> *Charles Garfield*

I tried to get every kid to spend even a few minutes thinking about what they want to do in life and what they need to do to get there. In class they didn't have time for this; what they heard was, "Open your book. Write a paper. Test on Thursday." Stuff like that. I felt they needed to be motivated, so that's what I tried to do. I got students to write down their personal mission statement, and I told them that this is their roadmap to life. I shared with them my roadmap, which I review and adjust each year as needed. Today my mission statement reads:

I am a God-fearing man full of integrity, honesty, and

patience. I am a loving, kind, supportive, and understanding husband to my wife. I am sensitive to the needs of my children, rearing them with the love of Jesus Christ and being supportive in their schoolwork and extracurricular activities, showing the love of Jesus Christ in everything I do and dedicating my life wholeheartedly to helpful and needy causes.

Every day I live by these words. I tell kids and adults alike that they, too, need to have a mission statement to guide them in life. I tell them, "You have to have a plan and a desire to fulfill that plan. Nobody knows what is in your heart but you. You have to develop a career based not on money, but on your heart." When a person does what he or she loves, eventually the money will come along. First and foremost is using our God-given abilities to do what we feel passionate and purposeful about. That comes first.

Helping Sam

I was making my rounds in the golf cart when Sam, a 12th grader, came up to me, his head down as he tried to hide his eyes swollen and bloodshot from crying. "What's up, man?" I asked.

He shook his head and said, "I don't know what I'm doing here."

"Well, son, you're here to get an education. That's what you're doing here."

"No, Mr. Marshall, that's not what I mean. I don't know why I *exist*."

Oh, that's another matter altogether. "Get in the golf cart, Sam, let's talk." As we drove around school that day, he opened up to me. I asked him about his relationship with his father. It turned out that his dad, a prominent real estate agent, was big on promises but short on delivery. He'd promise to take Sam fishing only to break that promise and go golfing with friends instead. His father did this sort of thing to him over and over again, to the point where young Sam felt confused, betrayed, and unappreciated. He felt like a nobody.

> Three billion people on the face of the earth go to bed hungry every night, but four billion people go to bed every night hungry for a simple word of encouragement and recognition.
>
> *Cavett Robert*

I listened, and then I explained that it wasn't his fault that his father behaved this way. I told Sam that sometimes a father can be home but still be absentee. I told him that now I understood why he acted up in class; it had everything to do with his deep desire for a relationship with his dad. Since it didn't look like that relationship would ever become what the son wanted, I tried to redirect Sam towards his own life, his future.

"Listen, Sam, this is what you've got to do," I said. "You need to figure out what is in your heart to do. Because you know, jails are full of kids your age, and even people younger than you. But you don't want to become that statistic. We have enough kids who are a menace to society, and we don't need more. You don't want to go that route. You have to find in your heart what it is that you have to do. Figure out, Sam, what you want to do with your life."

We talked some more, and he seemed a little better. By the time he stepped off the golf cart and walked back to class, he was much calmer. I said a prayer for this young man that day, and I prayed for him many times afterwards, even though we didn't get the chance to talk again. I hoped and prayed things would go well for Sam.

A year ago I walked into the local Home Depot to pick up a few items for a home repair project. A familiar-looking young man ran up to me and shook my hand. It took me less than a second to recognize him. Sam looked terrific, full of confidence and dignity, not the battered, confused teen I'd seen several years ago. "Mr. Marshall," he said, "I want to thank you. I'm in my second year in dental college. I'm making straight A's. I want to thank you for your words of encouragement when I was down." We both beamed at each other.

"I'm so glad to hear it, Sam," I replied. "I know you're going to be a powerful dentist, and I know you're going to help people. You have a wonderful opportunity to impact lives by doing what you enjoy. I'm proud of you."

Stop The Violence

We went through a period in our county when we experienced an epidemic of violent tragedies, including kids killing kids. Many of our students were personally affected by the violence. This situation was unacceptable...but how to stop it?

One morning I heard a group of kids singing rap songs just outside my classroom. I called them in. We talked a bit, then I said, "Listen, I know the shootings and killings have affected you personally. You've lost people you know and care about to gunfire. But it doesn't have to keep being this way. You guys can make a difference. You can use your talent, your voices, to do something to help stop the violence."

I had their attention. They stared at me, wondering where I was going with this. "Okay, here's the thing," I continued. "What I would do right now is take you guys to a recording studio, if you can write some songs about stopping the gun violence. Now I don't want to hear any swearing or cursing. I want to hear something uplifting and positive. Can you do it?"

> There is no meaning to life except the meaning man gives his life by the unfolding of his powers. To "maximize our potential," we must take advantage of the resources available designed to increase our understanding of ourselves, the people around us and the life we are now involved in. We become what we indulge ourselves in. The opportunities life offers help us tap our potential and can be explored when we are equipped with the right tools.
>
> *Erich Fromm*

Their eyes lit up. "You mean it, Mr. Marshall? You'll take us to a recording studio?" they asked, losing their mean, tough-guy exteriors. They weren't exactly model students. All of them were a bit of a menace to the school. But all of a sudden they were interested in doing something positive and productive. They agreed to do it.

Once they composed their songs, I took them, seven boys and one girl, to a recording studio. They named their group *Alter8tion,* and let me tell you, these kids sang their hearts out in that recording studio. I spent $7,000 of my own money to make it happen, but it was worth it. I sent their "Stop The Violence" CD to schools and radio stations across Palm Beach County and throughout the nation. These eight kids got air time on radio stations across America. They went on to perform at many schools and churches. To this day, their CD is used in our local school system.

Occasionally people ask me what I got out of it. It's true that I didn't make even a dime off this venture, but money was never my goal. My desire was to do something to stop the rampant violence, and with God's help, I showed these eight students, kids others had given up on, that they have the power within themselves to find solutions. To create positive change. Even to motivate others. What I got out of the deal is the knowledge that I was able to help eight young people straighten their paths, who in turn went on to help thousands of other kids make good choices. *They* did it. I was the silent person in the background. I even appointed one of the eight to be the manager of the group. Truly, the whole project was *their* accomplishment.

One evening *Alter8tion* was performing at a church youth event when a man about my age approached me. There was a sense of urgency in his eyes as he spoke. "Are you their manager?" he asked after the group had sung one of their powerful songs from their "Stop The Violence" album.

> You never know when a moment and a few sincere words can have an impact on a life.
>
> *Zig Ziglar*

"No, sir," I replied. "I did take them to the recording studio, but that young man over there is the manager."

"Well, that song they just did really touched my heart." He paused a moment, collecting his thoughts. "Listen," he continued, "let me tell you something. I've been a gang-banger. But I don't want to do that anymore. I want to change my life."

I took this man over to the youth pastor and shared with the pastor what he'd just told me. They began talking, and soon this frightened gang-banger was receiving Christ as his savior. He transformed right before my eyes, with a sense of peace finally coming over him.

So that $7,000 I spent was well worth it. If nothing else, I know it changed this one person, and to me it was worth that one life. He looked like he'd been wandering in the wilderness, but hearing that song by *Alter8tion* made the difference for him, helping him take that first important step to becoming a new creation in Christ.

My Friend Bryan

Almost the entire time I worked for the school, my good friend Bryan Boysaw, an accomplished attorney, was trying to get me to join him at his law firm. Bryan is someone I've admired since I was a kid. I've always looked up to him and thought of him as a big brother. As much as

I loved working at the school, the opportunity to work with Bryan and learn from him became too good to pass up. The time came when I felt I had accomplished a great deal in my various school roles, had motivated and encouraged many students, and had made a difference across the nation by facilitating *Alter8tion*. I gave myself permission to leave my job at the high school and go to work with my dear friend.

I reached the next level of my personal development by working with Bryan. He taught me about checks and balances, about dotting the i's and crossing the t's. I was used to being spontaneous and half-winging things, but he taught me to be meticulous and mind even the smallest of details. In a law firm, you have to catch and fix a mistake before it's ever made. There is no room for error when you're going before a judge to present a case.

My job at the firm was to investigate cases. I gathered evidence, took photos and measurements, and my findings either made or broke a case. It's a lot of responsibility for one person to have, and I thank God that Bryan put that level of trust in me. He would never hesitate to ask me, "What do you think?" I'd let him know whether or not I felt a case was solid.

Bryan also put me in charge of advertising and promotions. This was a new area for me, so I studied up to do things right. I had free reign. As long as I brought in clients and made sure they had what they needed, I was doing my job right.

> You may have the loftiest goals, the highest ideals, the noblest dreams, but remember this nothing works unless you do.
>
> *Nido Qubein*

Thankfully, I still got to work with youth. Schools were calling me, asking me to give motivational talks to their students. Bryan graciously allowed me to keep doing this. He also had me run one of his fun community projects. Every year, his law firm rewarded elementary school students from some of the local schools. Those who passed Florida's comprehensive assessment test, the FCAT, were treated to a movie event. My job was to make it happen. I had to select a movie, make arrangements with the theater, get the kids special T-shirts, secure transportation for them to and from the theater, and make sure everything ran smoothly. It was a huge job, but it was a blast!

Like I said before, working for Bryan taught me to mind the details, something no formal education could have given me. And this refined skill has come in handy many, many times in every area of my life. Including my health.

Success Story

Frederick Douglass Patterson

Orphaned at the age of two, Frederick D. Patterson was voted "Least Likely To Succeed" when he was in the eighth grade. How wrong his classmates were. He earned his Doctorate of Veterinary Medicine from Iowa State and his Doctorate of Philosophy from Cornell University. In his autobiography, he wrote these very wise words: "How people feel about you reflects the way you permit yourself to be treated. If you permit yourself to be treated differently, you are condemned to an unequal relationship."

When he was thirty-three, Frederick was selected to become president of Tuskegee Institute, a role he served for nearly twenty-five years. Other accomplishments include:

- Grew the institute into a university with outstanding graduate programs
- Advanced the school's veterinarian and engineering programs
- Launched a commercial aviation program
- Started a program to train the first African American Air Corps pilots
- Pioneered practical, inexpensive house construction methods
- Continued to improve and enhance higher education throughout his entire life

- Was awarded the Presidential Medal of Freedom

But perhaps his greatest legacy is founding the United Negro College Fund, which has given thousands of young African Americans access to higher education. The man once voted "least likely to succeed" is responsible for helping countless young people succeed in education and in life. He shows us what can be accomplished when we follow our passion and refuse to listen to the doomsayers.

CHAPTER 11
Cured From Multiple Sclerosis

The wish of healing has always been half of health.
*Lucius Annaeus Seneca,
philosopher, statesman, dramatist*

Cured From Multiple Sclerosis

One day I was walking, just like any other day, when suddenly my left leg gave out from under me. *What was that about?* I asked myself. I shrugged it off and continued with my business. Quite a few people had been urging me to get more rest. My style was to go nonstop from the second I woke up to the moment I went to bed, trying to get as much accomplished during my waking hours as possible. I didn't sleep much, either. I figured I was just tired, that's all.

But then I started to notice other little things that weren't completely normal. For one, my eyes were having a difficult time focusing. Maybe I was developing a stigmatism? A trip to the optometrist revealed that my vision had changed, and I needed new glasses. When I went back a week later to pick them up, though, they weren't correct. My eyes had changed in just that short period of time! The doctor rechecked my eyes and had a different pair of glasses made for me. Even with the new pair, I still couldn't focus well. And every so often, when I least expected it, my legs continued to buckle underneath me.

I was scheduled to have surgery on my shoulder for a torn rotator cuff, a condition that first appeared when I was a young man playing baseball and had worsened through the years. Thankfully my surgery was a success and my recovery went well. My shoulder had healed to the point where I no longer needed the post-surgery pain medication, so I stopped taking it.

One Sunday morning not too long after my operation, I began to feel sharp pains in the region around my left temple. No matter what I did, I couldn't make the pain go away. Finally I tried the very strong pain medication the hospital had given me to take after my surgery. Even *that* didn't work! Nothing did.

The next day things got worse. When I closed my right eye, I noticed that the vision in my left eye was clouded. This really scared me. I told Kim about it. She dropped everything and drove me to the doctor, who took a look and explained that I had minor scarring. He told me it would heal on its own, and I'd be fine.

> You learn that, whatever you are doing in life, obstacles don't matter very much. Pain or other circumstances can be there, but if you want to do a job bad enough, you'll find a way to get it done.
>
> *Jack Youngblood*

Two days later, I could no longer see from my left eye. I went back to my doctor, who referred me to an ophthalmologist. Crying, Kim drove me straight there. After examining me and asking a few questions, the ophthalmologist gave me his verdict.

"It looks like you have multiple sclerosis, but you'll need to see a neurologist to make sure."

More Than Just Being Tired

A CAT scan and a spinal tap confirmed it: I had MS. In that split second when the neurologist delivered the news, an image of my wife and kids flashed in my mind, and I prayed: *Lord, I want to keep seeing them with both eyes.*

The doctor said I needed to go to the hospital immediately to be placed on anti-inflammatory medications administered through an IV drip. The goal was to reduce the inflammation around my optic nerve, which had swollen to the point where light could no longer come through. I understood the urgency of the situation. Any delay in getting treatment would mean permanent scarring and ultimately blindness in that eye.

The hospital, however, was completely booked. No beds available until next week, they told me. I didn't have the luxury of time. I called my good friend Dr. O, a leading specialist on infectious diseases.

"Listen, I need your help," I said, filling him in on the details. "Can I come to your office and have you perform the IV drip? I need to do this for the next seven days."

"Yes, I can do that, Aldric. Come on in."

> It may not be your fault for being down, but it's got to be your fault for not getting up.
>
> *Steve Davis*

Four hours every day for the next week, I sat with a group of AIDS patients, all of us hooked up to IVs. I saw this as an opportunity to motivate my new friends. "Nobody has control over your life except for you and God," I said. "They diagnosed me with MS after I lost my eyesight in my left eye. They may have diagnosed you with AIDS, and you may think that all hope is gone, but it doesn't have to be your reality. If you have a will to live, you will. But if your mind is consumed with negative thoughts, you're going to be depressed and weighed down, and then all hope is lost. When you fill your mind with positive affirmations and say to yourself, 'Come hell or high water, I'm gonna live,' you're gonna live."

Empowering Myself With Knowledge

Through my interaction with these courageous AIDS patients in Dr. O's office, I learned something. I discovered that when you stop thinking about what's going on with you and instead start helping others solve their problems, you begin to forget your own worries. When the neurologist confirmed that I had MS, I was stunned. How did I get it? What caused it? My doctor was just as stumped. He told me that within the medical community, MS is thought of as a disease that affects mainly young white females. How did I, an otherwise healthy black man, come down with MS?

I felt I had the weight of the world on my shoulders... until I sat down with these AIDS patients and started talking with them. Suddenly my problem felt so small compared to what the man sitting next to me with the IV pack on his arm was going through. This is what reaching out to others does for us. We forget our own problems for a moment as we strive to help our fellow man.

> I am grateful for all my problems. After each one was overcome, I became stronger and more able to meet those that were still to come. I grew in all my difficulties.
>
> *J. C. Penny*

Sure enough, my eyesight returned, and I thanked God for my restored vision. My neurologist put me on medication called Copaxone, which I had to inject into my body. By no means is this a cure. It merely inhibits further development of lesions in the brain (one of the symptoms of MS). The doctor cautioned that if I stopped taking this drug, I could relapse, with lesions starting to develop again. So every night I gave myself an injection. At $1,500 a month, the stuff wasn't cheap.

I asked if Copaxone would hurt my kidneys. Seeing my dad on dialysis as a direct result of doctors giving him one high blood pressure drug after another, I was somewhat distrustful of traditional medicine. I didn't want to take anything that would hurt my body; I especially didn't want my kidneys to fail. The doctor told me not to worry about it because my kidneys would be fine.

I turned to the Lord for answers. To me this was one giant puzzle, and with God's help I was going to unravel the mystery and learn how to get this mess out of my body. Prayer and knowledge, I felt, would lead to healing. Through prayer God told me to get on the Internet and start doing research. I did. I armed myself with information so I could make the best decisions possible for my health.

God Threw Me a Life Preserver

Have you ever heard this story? A man was sailing across the ocean when suddenly a giant wave came along and overturned his boat. The boat sank, and the man was left alone swimming for his life. He prayed, *Lord, please save me!* Soon a boat appeared and somebody threw him a life preserver. "Grab it!" the crew yelled while their vessel bounced around on the choppy seas.

"No thanks!" said the man. "I'm waiting for the Lord to save me."

The boat left, and the man continued to pray. Soon another boat appeared, and a second life preserver was hurled towards him. But again, he refused to take it. "The Lord will save me!"

Then a rescue helicopter came to the scene, dropping a long rope ladder directly over the man. All he had to do was reach up and grab it. But he refused. "No thanks," he yelled. "God's gonna save me!"

Suddenly, over the sound of the sea and the loud hum

of the copter blades, a booming voice came down from the heavens. It was the Lord's voice: "Listen, I'm trying to help you. I've thrown you two life preservers and a rope ladder, but you keep rejecting me. What do I have to do to get your attention?"

I was that guy in the open sea, rejecting the life preserver God tossed my way, when I wouldn't listen to my close friend who tried to help me.

"Listen," my friend confided, "I had developing signs of prostate cancer. So I went over to a homeopathic doctor and followed his regimen. I realize it may be hard to believe, but after going through his treatments for a while, I went back to my traditional doctor to get checked and see if the alternative treatments were doing anything. He was amazed—I had *no* more signs of cancer! They simply vanished. Aldric, you *need* to go see this guy."

> Too often, the opportunity knocks, but by the time you push back the chain, push back the bolt, unhook the two locks, and shut off the burglar alarms, it's too late.
>
> *Rita Coolidge*

I was ecstatic for my friend and his excellent diagnosis. But I wasn't convinced about the homeopathic doctor. There had to be another explanation for his miraculous cure. It couldn't have been the alternative health treatment. I just didn't buy into that kind of stuff. I thanked him for his concern and went back to my hunt for the root cause of my health issues.

This friend, however, was persistent. Very persistent. He kept pressing me, stopping by the barber shop at all hours, pushing me to see his alternative health doctor. "Al, I want you to go down there," he insisted. I told him I'd think about it, but that wasn't good enough for him. "I'm going to keep talking to you and Kim until you go see him!"

His persistence won. I ended up calling my friend's doctor, if nothing else to get him to leave me alone. The doctor and his wife ran their homeopathic practice out of their home. As soon as I walked inside and met the man, I knew he was full of the love of God. Finally I began to see what my persistent friend was talking about. This physician took the time to really talk with me about my condition. He asked question after question to gather as much information as possible, and he did so with obvious compassion and respect. He was so conscientious and honest. I decided to give him a try. What did I have to lose?

Many of my friends were skeptical about alternative health treatments, just as I had been. Some were downright negative towards this doctor. "He's a quack!" they insisted. "He's going to mess you up, Aldric. Don't listen to him. You need to see a real doctor."

I have to admit that for a while I was torn. I didn't know what to do. But I knew one thing: I was tired of those nightly injections that left me bruised and sore. I didn't want to take Copaxone for the rest of my life. I kept praying to the Lord to deliver me out of this, to heal me. I leaned completely on God to help me. His answer came clearly, like a life preserver in my big ocean of confusion... *work with the homeopathic doctor.* I listened.

A New Approach

My new doctor looked at my health issues with a completely open mind. He explored all angles, taking nothing for granted. I was floored when he stated to me, without a trace of ego, "What you're suffering with is easily curable." Wow! Nobody had *ever* told me that before. The traditional doctors had given me a life sentence, so to speak. Now, for the first time since being diagnosed with MS, I was given hope for a cure!

"We can take care of what you have and make you better," he insisted. "But first, you will need to have the amalgam fillings removed from your mouth. They're causing mercury poisoning in your system. I can't do anything until you have them removed. If you start treatments before removing the fillings, it's no different than putting new wine into old wineskin."

Wow. All this was new to me. The mercury in my mouth poisoning my body—I'd never heard of such a thing. I had a few options, the doctor informed me. I could have the procedure done in the U.S., where it came with a huge price tag, or I could go to the Santa Monica Health Institute in Baja, Mexico, which specialized in amalgam removal and many other complementary medicine modalities. I had a lot to consider. I got back on the Internet and started researching everything from mercury poisoning to the clinic in Mexico.

> By exposing yourself to risk, you're exposing yourself to heavy-duty learning, which gets you on all levels. It becomes a very emotional experience as well as an intellectual experience. Each time you make a mistake, you're learning from the school of hard knocks, which is the best education available.
>
> *Gifford Pinchot*

I came to realize that my new doctor was right; the mercury in my mouth was definitely hurting me. To this day I find it incredible that dentists are still allowed to fill cavities using mercury amalgam. When you break a thermometer, which is filled with mercury, you have to be extra careful. Don't vacuum the mercury because you'll disperse it through the air, increasing your exposure to this poisonous element. Don't sweep it up because you'll break the mercury into smaller droplets and spread it around more. Don't pour it down the drain, as it could pollute the sewage treatment plant!

With all of these don'ts and the obvious toxicity of mercury, I can't understand why dental professionals put mercury in our mouths, in our teeth, sitting right atop an important branch of the body's nervous system. Every time you bite down on something, you release mercury into your nervous system. You are poisoning your body, day after day, year after year. After learning all of this, I knew that I wanted my fillings out, as well as Kim's. There was no question about it; if I had this procedure done because it was the best thing health-wise, Kim would have it done as well. I love my wife deeply. How could I live with myself knowing that her health might be deteriorating because we failed to take preventive action?

I was apprehensive about going to the clinic in Mexico, so I began by calling several doctors in the United States. The most reasonably priced one charged $9,000 per person to remove the existing fillings and replace them with porcelain. Multiply this figure by two, and that's a lot of money that Kim and I just didn't have. The Mexican clinic could do the very same procedure for a fraction of the cost. Santa Monica Health Institute was starting to look a lot more appealing.

> What this power is I cannot say; all I know is that it exists and it becomes available only when a man is in that state of mind in which he knows exactly what he wants and is fully determined not to quit until he finds it.
>
> *Alexander Graham Bell*

Again, friends and family members were concerned. "Don't go down there," they insisted. "We'll help you pay for it so you can get the procedure done stateside." I appreciated their offer, but by then I'd already researched the clinic thoroughly and felt comfortable with the quality of their services. Kim and I arranged to travel to the hospital in Baja.

Santa Monica Health Institute

It was a homely hospital perched along the coast,

overlooking the deep-blue Pacific Ocean. A driver picked us up in a van and drove us to the clinic, along the way sharing stories about patients. "I've met a lot of people who come here for what you're having done," he explained. "And people with many other conditions. People come in with cancer, Lyme disease, you name it. When they arrive, they can barely walk. Soon, they're walking around, their cancer shrunk to undetectable levels. What you have, sir, I see all the time being taken care of here. No problem."

We pulled into the hospital, a converted hotel, along a dirt road as dogs scurried away. Kim and I thanked our driver and walked inside where we saw nurses, doctors, and patients walking around, the medical staff taking care of folks. Nurses came up to greet us, and we were led into a room to begin our chelation intravenous drip, a cleansing technique meant to protect us from any possible contact with the mercury amalgam fillings being extracted. About four hours later, we were done. We walked back to the lobby area where we heard testimony after testimony from patients who were getting better. We heard them say how God had led them down this path to heal their bodies through natural, holistic regiments.

> The people who are playing it totally safe are never going to have either the fun or the rewards of the people who decide to take some risk, stick out, do it differently.
>
> *John Akers*

I spent some time chatting with a young girl who had been wheeled in with Lyme disease and now was walking on her own. I met a man from Barbados who had flown in to get treatment for cancer. He told me that he was about ready to leave, with the cancerous tumor having shrunk to an undetectable size. Kim and I spent hours listening to stories people shared with us, their personal tales of recovering from cancer, multiple sclerosis, AIDS, and many other ailments. We felt we were in the midst of miracles. Truly, Kim and I were humbled.

And I couldn't help but think that it's a shame we had to leave our nation and head sixteen miles into Mexico for a treatment that we very well could have received in our own United States, had it not been for greed and an excessive focus on "the bottom line." At this Mexican clinic, the doctors and nurses didn't make a whole lot of money. They didn't have insurance companies paying them big bucks. And yet, not once did they try to sell us anything. They performed what we came for with efficiency, respect, and compassion.

Later on, as we explored this little Mexican city with the help of our cab driver, he asked for just $5, but we gave him $25. I looked around and noticed that even though the people here didn't have much, they were content. He showed us the real Baja, away from the tourist areas. These folks didn't have the amenities and commodities we enjoy in the U.S., but it was evident they had heart. As I like to say, it's not so much what you have, but what you do with what you have. With the little bit these folks had, they were happy. No Mercedes or Volvos but modest little cars that did the job and the people were satisfied with. Our kind cab driver drove us all over, and we were very grateful to him. What we saw drew my wife and me closer together, because we realized we had so much in the United States, and we were appreciative.

> To feel compassion is to feel that we are in some sort and to some extent responsible for the pain that is being inflicted, that we ought to do something about it.
>
> *Aldous Huxley*

When it was time for us to leave, I didn't want to go. I had met so many wonderful new friends in our brief time here. We had arrived on a Tuesday and were leaving that Thursday. But our eye-opening journey had come to an end, and we flew back to Florida with a new perspective on health, on giving from the heart, and on being truly grateful for the countless blessings we have.

A Holistic Method

I went back to my holistic doctor. With the amalgams out of my body, he was ready to start me on his program. He put me on colonics, a system of total purging. I learned that what we eat, especially in our fast-food diets lacking in fresh fruits, vegetables, and fiber, clogs our digestive system to the point where food can't pass through our intestines in an efficient, timely manner. Do you know that we're actually supposed to have a bowel movement following every meal? I didn't. This was all new to me.

Nobody had ever taught me these things in health class. So the colonics flushed my system out.

> The poorest man will not part with health for money, but...the richest would gladly part with all their money for health.
>
> *C. C. Colton*

God designed the body to expel all impurities through various ingenious methods—through our urine and bowel movements, obviously, and through our pores via sweating, and even through our nostrils when we have a cold. Yet we seem determined to keep those impurities in. We fail to drink enough water or consume foods that keep us regular. When we have a cold, we take medicines to prevent us from sneezing and having runny noses. We do everything we can to keep from sweating. In the process of our modern-day living, we keep toxins inside and make ourselves sick. When we eat the wrong foods and get stopped up, we end up with higher blood pressure, headaches, fogginess in our mind, and other unpleasant symptoms. Why? Because all of the waste that needs to come out is lodged inside our intestines, and our bloodstream circulates these toxins to every part of our body. It's so important to stay regular. Every system in our body benefits from healthy intestines.

I changed my diet. The doctor had me consume plenty of raw foods, especially vegetables and fruits, as well as natural, freshly made juices. This holistic approach was working; after only a week, I felt so much better already—less bloated, more energized, and with a sharper mind. On this regimen, I lost twenty pounds in seven days, without feeling weakened or deprived in any way. On the contrary, I felt renewed and stronger than ever.

He gave me a list of what to do at home. I followed it completely. I stopped drinking sodas, which are terrible for us because of the excessive sugar content and the carbon dioxide. I continued to adjust my diet to eat right. I took enzymes to rebuild the population of beneficial bacteria in my body that penicillin had destroyed. I could feel my body healing itself. I could feel my strength returning and the pain diminishing. With the onset of MS, I had been experiencing severe back pains. My feet would ache so badly. But with this holistic approach prescribed by my alternative medicine doctor, the pain lessened. Every day I felt better. After two months on my new regimen, I felt deep in my soul that it was time. I felt I was healed. I took myself off Copaxone, because in my heart and in my soul, I felt I no longer had a need for it.

> Health is not valued till sickness comes.
>
> *Thomas Fuller*

Instead of putting harsh medications into myself, I put things into my body to rebuild my immune system, rebuild my nervous system, and cleanse my digestive system and my blood. The Bible tells us in 1 Corinthians that our body is the temple of the Holy Ghost, and that we are to glorify God in our body. That's exactly what I was doing. I was treating my body as a temple, treating it right for the glory of God. I stayed away from eating fish because of high levels of mercury in the water. I ate all-natural, organic foods only, free of pesticides and other harmful chemicals. Yes, it's expensive, but I felt I couldn't afford to *not* do it. My wife, our children, and I had never eaten more healthful foods, and all of us felt so much better than ever. I'd rather pay a little more and put quality food on our table than have to spend that money on medications. I'd rather eat fresh, wholesome foods than pop pills any day!

Cured

Meanwhile, I continued to see my regular medical doctor for checkups. I didn't tell him that I had taken myself off Copaxone because, frankly, I didn't want him chewing me out. I just went to get checked out and see how I was progressing. He administered blood tests and, every time, he told me everything was fine. *So far, so good,* I thought. After I'd been off the prescribed medications for a year, I finally confessed to my doctor.

"Are you still on the medication, Aldric?"

"No, sir, I haven't been on it for a year. And I have to tell you, I feel fine. I am healed of MS."

He looked skeptical. "Well, I've got to send you in for a CAT scan."

That was different. "Not a blood test this time?" I asked.

"No, that was just to check your kidneys, to make sure nothing goes wrong."

I couldn't believe what I'd just heard. My kidneys?

After he had assured me the medications would not and could not hurt my kidneys? I couldn't hide my anger.

"Hold on a moment. When you put me on Copaxone, you said it would *not* affect my kidneys. Now you're telling me that all those blood tests were to see if my kidneys were getting damaged? What am I supposed to believe?"

He defended himself, telling me that because I'd been on it for a period of time, he had to check. It was routine.

"Well," I replied, "I am glad I'm off this medicine, because when I was on it I felt horrible! I'm glad I took myself off."

I agreed to go in for the CAT scan, but I left telling my doctor, "I don't know what you're looking for, because I'm healed."

> The trouble with advice is that you can't tell if it's good or bad until you've taken it.
>
> *Frank Tyger*

A week after my CAT scan, my doctor called me back in. I noticed that he had two images in front of him and an astonished look on his face.

"Aldric," he began, "I don't know what you're doing, exactly, but I have to tell you, in all my years as a doctor, I've never seen this before." He showed me both images, comparing the one I'd just taken with the one that was done when I was first diagnosed with MS.

"Generally," he continued, "when a person goes off of the MS medications, the lesions come right back.

But look, there are no new lesions. None whatsoever. Whatever you're doing, Aldric, keep doing it, because it's working."

Trust In God

It's been four years now since I was cured of multiple sclerosis, and the lesions have not returned. The mind is a powerful thing. Don't disregard your healing; embrace it! Believe in it. The process of healing is not that different from going to any type of anonymous support group. First, you must acknowledge that there is a problem. You can't deny it, because if you do, then you fail to face it. So speak your problem, and then put a solution to your problem. You don't have to put ownership on your illness or ailment, but you do have to recognize that you are diagnosed with this condition.

> Then he said to him, "Rise and go; your faith has made you well."
>
> *Luke* 17:19, NIV

I recognized that I had MS and that it was present, but I did not take ownership of it. The next step after recognition is knowing that, just as you have the problem, you also have the solution through Jesus Christ. Instead of taking ownership, I turned it over to Jesus and in his name asked that he heal my body. With my mouth, I spoke these words every chance I got: *They diagnosed me with MS, but by Jesus' might I am healed.*

The Bible tells us to ask, and it shall be given. So ask boldly. Don't waver. First, recognize what you have in order to be healed by God from what you have. Then, have the confidence that what you've asked for is being given. Believe that you are being healed, and don't look back!

Success Story

Joni Eareckson Tada, Christian Author, Artist, & Disability Advocate

As founder and CEO of Joni And Friends, a Christian organization that advocates for and empowers the disabled, Joni Eareckson Tada devotes herself to serving God by making sure the Gospel of Jesus Christ reaches all people with disabilities and their families. Her heart is truly in her work, and she knows firsthand many of the challenges that having a disability can create. When she was a teenager, a diving accident resulted in her breaking her neck and becoming a quadriplegic. She lost the use of her limbs, but she learned to compensate in many ways. Joni learned how to paint by holding a brush with her mouth. She also taught herself how to achieve some movement in her arms by using her back and shoulder muscles; this enabled her to learn to drive in a modified car.

Having overcome many challenges and finding church to be a tremendous support for her and her family, she decided to help others in similar situations. After writing her autobiography and sharing her story with the world through her book and countless speaking engagements, Joni launched her ministry, Joni And Friends, back in 1979, and it's still going strong today. She has written a total of thirty-two books to date, and continues to paint. She and her husband, Ken, are passionate about inspiring disabled individuals to live a full, Christ-centered life. She also strives to help churches become more inclusive of the disabled. In addition to running her organization and its many programs, Joni inspires a million people every week through her daily radio program. She shows all of us that regardless of our limitations and challenges, we can live to our full potential and use the gifts God gave us to help one another.

CHAPTER 12
Building Healthy Lives, Healthy Communities

The person who gets the farthest is generally the one who is willing to do and dare.

The sure-thing boat never gets far from shore.

Dale Carnegie,
writer, lecturer, course developer

Building Healthy Lives, Healthy Communities

October 31st, 2007, Halloween. Nearly a thousand kids, from pre-teens to older teenagers, gathered for a common cause. Not for trick-or-treating. Not for a wild Halloween bash. They were gathered at an event I had organized as a healthy alternative to whatever else they might be doing that night. Certainly they were there for fun, to socialize with others their age, and for the free food, but more importantly, they were there to take stock of their lives and decide where they were headed. Our primary common goal was to turn back on rap and turn forward to Christ.

The entire community was involved. Businesses contributed to make this event happen. Churches helped out with facilitating the event. We had plenty of free food for the kids and everyone who attended. We had inspiring guest speakers who roused these young people and challenged them to do something positive with their lives.

We got them to first think about the lyrics they were listening to in their rap music and then decide to start listening to music more responsibly. People of all colors attended. The best part was about four hundred fifty people received Christ that night. It was amazing.

I organized this event as part of my new mission, Urban Youth Development, an initiative I launched with my wife. Technically, I began this effort ten years ago, but it went by a different name. Back then I called it "Men On A Mission," and it involved Monday night sessions at the barber shop to help young men, many who came from broken homes, become responsible, righteous individuals with a passion for God and a desire to do the right thing. It all started very informally with their mothers coming to the shop and asking, "Mr. Al, can you talk to my son about his schoolwork?" Or about staying out of trouble, minding his manners, staying away from drugs...just about anything. Of course, I always honored these mother's requests and spoke earnestly to their sons. But there came a point when I knew I had to take it to the next level, so I dedicated Monday evenings to the "Men On A Mission" mentoring program I designed.

> Everybody can be great...because anybody can serve. You don't have to have a collage degree to serve. You don't have to make your subject and verb agree to serve...You only need a heart of grace, a soul generated by love.
>
> *Dr. Martin Luther King, Jr.*

Ten years later Kim and I revamped this concept, creating a new model and calling it Urban Youth Development. Mind you, I never stopped mentoring and motivating youth. In the past decade I've mentored countless young men, guiding them on everything from eating a nutritious diet to getting an education to following their dreams. I've helped a pro athlete condition himself to stay fit by staying before God, praying, working out, keeping his body healthy, and most importantly, keeping his focus on God to stay on the right path and avoid getting distracted by temptations.

I've encouraged many young men to attend college. Young men like Zach and Morris, who were in my Men On A Mission program. It makes me extremely proud to know that they are in the MBA program at FAMU University. These guys are doing exceptionally well. I still remember when they were sitting here at the barber shop, sharing with me that they were planning to go to college to learn how to make money legitimately. They never let go of their dreams, and look where they are today. Whenever they come home, they always stop by to say hello. And they invariably ask me, "Mr. Marshall, when will you start the Men On A Mission program again?" My reply is always the same: I will restart the program when they come help me.

In the meantime, I am focused on Urban Youth Development (UYD). Kim and I have created a new paradigm that we hope will reach more young men and get a larger segment of the community involved. Our goal is to get these urban youth to dream and realize that with hope, persistence, God, and community, they *can* do it! They can be successful in business and in life.

Here where I live, there are approximately 166,000 businesses. And yet, only about 6.5% are owned and run by minorities. That's under 11,000 businesses. I'd like to see this picture change, and UYD is my way of making a difference. UYD goes beyond a basic mentoring program. It strives to help young people get fired up about owning and securing their own destiny, because it's an *entrepreneur* mentoring program. We teach both at-risk and not at-risk kids how to become entrepreneurs. We do this by teaching them basic business principles, building character, showing them minority role models in the business community, and supporting their efforts. Kim and I are just getting started with this venture, and we're very excited by the potential to empower youth. We want these kids to know that they *can* become business owners. I am convinced that everyone, regardless of background, education, or economic level, can start and run their own successful business.

> The people who are crazy enough to think they can change the world are the ones who do.
>
> *Apple Computer, Inc.*

I was fortunate because growing up, I had a fantastic role model—my mom. She was a business owner, first with her own stylist's chair and later with her own salon. I knew it was possible because I watched her do it. Through UYD, I hope to have every urban youth see that business ownership is a real possibility. Everyone wants to be a sports figure or a rap star because our present-day culture tells them these are the only roles in which they can succeed. I want to change that misperception. I'm here to tell them that they can be successful in anything they put their mind to.

I'm here to expand their minds and give them additional role models like Garrett Augustus Morgan, an African-American inventor who patented one of the first automatic traffic signals, which he later sold to General Electric. Or Fredrick Jones, an African-American garage mechanic who invented the first automatic refrigeration system for long-haul trucks. Or Kenneth Irvine Chenault, also African American, who's been the CEO and Chairman of American Express, recently ranked #79 among Fortune 500 companies, since 2001. I want young men to learn about important role models such as these and realize that they, too, can become successful business owners, inventors, innovators, and entrepreneurs.

When I meet with UYD kids, I tell them this: *I don't care if you are blind, are in a wheelchair, are educationally challenged, have absentee parents, have been abused, or have dropped out of school, you can start a business! There is a business for you if you want to put blood, sweat, and effort behind it. We'll meet you where you're at. We'll help you. We'll develop your strengths and work on your weaknesses so that you can move forward and move up. You can do it!*

> We can learn to soar only in direct proportion to our determination to rise above the doubt and transcend the limitations.
>
> *David McNally*

Empowering Youth

I don't have to tell you that kids are the most silent people in America. Even today, they are told verbally and non-verbally that they should be "seen and not heard." They try to talk, but we admonish, "Don't interrupt me. I'm talking." This makes me very sad, because I remember what it was like when I was a kid. And I want to stress to you that kids want to engage in meaningful conversation, just like adults do. We stop them by not allowing them to communicate.

Maybe youth have different things to say than adults do, but they still have things to say, and they want to be heard. They want to be active participants in a conversation. And it's good for them to participate. It gives them self-esteem, builds their speaking abilities, and motivates them to articulate using proper words. When you teach children upper-level communication skills, they will speak eloquently and confidently.

Empower youth and you ignite a fire.

I try to involve my kids in both conversation and decision-making. How do we expect young people to learn these important skills if we don't give them room to practice? When I was making decisions regarding the production of this book, for example, I engaged my son, Kaleb, who is eight years old. I showed him several books and asked him, "Would you buy a hardcover or a soft-cover book?" Just to allow him to engage in the process meant a lot to him.

One of my jobs is a consultant to churches, and

my son accompanies me to all of the training sessions I host. He helps me set up the projector and is my general assistant.

My daughter Keturah, who is six years old, helps me even before I leave the house. She's my fashion consultant. I ask for her opinion on my wardrobe. "Daddy, that doesn't match," she might tell me, and I listen. Or she may say, "Dad, that looks good," and I trust her judgment.

As a father, it's so important that you involve your children in your everyday life. The four of us—Kim, Kaleb, Keturah, and I are in this thing together. We work as a family, we spend time together as a family, and we pray together. And on that rare occasion when we're in a rush and I forget to pray, my son will remind me that we forgot to. Sure enough, we stop everything, and we pray.

> Children who are not spoken to by... responsive adults will not learn to speak properly. Children who are not answered will stop asking questions. They will become incurious. And children who are not told stories and who are not read to will have few reasons for wanting to learn to read.
>
> *Gail Haley*

You know that I have a passion for helping youth. I hope that you, too, will work towards empowering our young people. This could mean taking the time to listen to a young person speak, mentoring a child, volunteering at a school once a week, teaching Sunday school, or just being there for the kids and teens in your life. When you invest in a child, you help create a better world today and a stronger tomorrow.

But the needs out there are many, and you can use your abilities to help others in countless ways. The elderly need our help. So do the economically disadvantaged, the ill, people with disabilities, people in prison, people without a home, people with serious illnesses. You can help your community in countless ways. I urge you to get out there, roll up your sleeves, and help your fellow human in some way. Not only will you be assisting another person, you also will be rewarded greatly knowing that you've done something to improve your community and our world.

Connecting The World

Another ministry God has given me is called "Connecting The World With The Word Ministries" (God gave me the name for it, too). It's all about connecting the people of the world with the Word of God. It is a teaching ministry that shows the people, the body of Christ, how to go out into the world and be effective Christians and believers of God. As Ephesians 4:11–13 NIV states:

It was he who gave some to be apostles, some to be prophets, some to be evangelists, and some to be pastors and teachers, to prepare God's people for works of service, so that the body of Christ may be built up until we all reach unity in the faith and in the knowledge of the Son of God and become mature, attaining to the whole measure of the fullness of Christ.

> Live a life geared to helping others and the gears will start to shift for you.

The goal of "Connecting The World" is to build up the body of Christ. I teach about evangelism, how to get captives back, going behind enemy lines, how to get people who are dead in the world to come to know Christ. My heart is invested in this ministry. This is the only pyramid or multi-level marketing I'll ever get involved with! I teach you, and you teach someone else, then he or she teaches somebody else, and it continues to trickle forward, reaching more people than one person alone possibly could. When that 100,000th person comes to Christ, I'll know that I will have had my hand in that. This is what we're called to do: to share the love and message of Christ. I take this very seriously.

Success Story

Ephren Taylor

At only twenty-three, Ephren W. Taylor II became CEO of City Capital Corporation, an investment company specializing in "Socially-Conscious Investing To Empower Urban Communities," as his company website states. This accomplishment made him the youngest African American CEO of any publicly traded company in the United States. Can you guess how old he was when he started his first company? Brace yourself... Ephren was just twelve years old when he launched a company to design video games! He then created a job search portal for teens and moved on to launch a ventures company that helped fund churches and other nonprofits.

At such a young age, Ephren is already a sought-after lecturer and teacher, as well as a wise mentor. He teaches about economic empowerment and works toward positive change in urban communities. In 2002, the Kansas Department of Commerce awarded him the Young Entrepreneur Of The Year Award. Ephren is all about creating win-win situations for communities and his investors by thinking outside of the box and creating beneficial partnerships. Ephren proves that you don't have to wait until you're in your forties or fifties to become a successful entrepreneur.

CHAPTER 13
The Keys To Overcome Your Scars

> Out of suffering have emerged the strongest souls;
> The most massive characters are seared with scars.
>
> *Kahlil Gibran,*
> *essayist, novelist, poet, artist*

The Keys To Overcome Your Scars

Within the pages of this book, I have shared with you how I took the scars that life has given me and used them to move forward and achieve success. By no means am I extraordinary, though. I'm just an ordinary fellow. So if I can overcome the scars and achieve success, why not you?

Hope

One thing you'll need is hope. With hope in your heart, you can always imagine a better future, a better existence, and then work towards that vision. Hope enables you to dream, to move forward, to rise up after every mistake or failure and keep going.

Some years ago I read about a remarkable young woman attempting to swim the English Channel. As she started to swim, with the crew around her for protection, the skies became dark and the waters grew choppy. Soon a full-blown storm was raging, with lightning and huge swells. Halfway through her swim, she stopped and waved a crewmember over. "I can't do this," she said. They picked her up into the boat, and her attempt that day ended.

Some time later, she jumped back into the channel and tried again. This time, not only did she complete her swim, but she did it in record-breaking time. When the news media met her on the shore, reporters asked her what made the difference—how was she able to succeed this time? She answered that before jumping into the water, she looked at the shore across the way and had hope burned into her mind and spirit, hope that this time, she *would* make it.

> Hope begins in the dark, the stubborn hope that if you just show up and try to do the right thing, the dawn will come. You wait and watch and work: you don't give up.
>
> *Anne Lamott*

Like this courageous young woman, you're going to have the storms. The rain's gonna fall, distractions will come along, and some people will try to discourage you. But if you can disregard these things and keep the one main thing that'll get you there on your mind, you'll succeed. If you can focus on where you are going and what you are trying to reach, the storms won't bother you.

Persecution won't matter. Failure will be no more than a learning experience, a stepping stone to bring you closer to success. All that matters is that with focus and dedication, you're going to arrive victorious at the other end. That, my friends, is hope.

Persistence

I don't believe you can have hope without persistence. The two go hand in hand. Each of us already has a built-in mechanism of persistence within us. The question is: do we know how to use it? Do we tap into it when we need to? It's true that sometimes this mechanism gets cobwebs, but it's up to each of us to dust it off and put it to good use. Remember, you are a human being designed for greatness. Don't let a roadblock keep you back—find a way around, through, or over that roadblock! Be persistent.

The hope and persistence duo wakes you up each morning with the words, "Come on, man, you've got to go!" This dynamic duo helps each of us prevent the world from stealing our dreams, goals, and ambitions. When you want something badly enough, and you have that hope and optimism that you will reach your goal, you'll get it.

I think of persistence in particular as a compass giving you the direction that you need. It keeps you on course, whatever your goal may be. Without exception, everybody has it... although it's true that some folks have more persistence than others. It's equally true that wherever you may be on the persistence scale, you can grow in this important attribute through both your attitude and your actions. Everybody has that winning spirit that catapults them to the next level, and everybody can become more and more persistent through practice and tenacity.

> The one who gives up will never see the fullness persistence has for them.

My advice to you is this: Don't let anyone take away your persistence through their vain words that aren't true. Someone's comments about you do *not* have to be your reality! Regardless of what others say, just keep driving. Keep going one step at a time. Keep pushing forward. Trust that you *will* get there.

When I was a little kid, I didn't like having my mother out of sight. As soon as she'd go into the restroom and close that door—probably the only moment of privacy she had all day long—I was knocking on the door. "Open the door, Momma, I want to talk to you!"

"I'll be out in a minute, son."

"Momma, I want to tell you something. Open the door!"

"Just a moment, Aldric!"

"Open the door, please, Momma!"

Finally, the door swung open and there stood Momma. "What is it, child? What do you need to tell me?"

"I just want to tell you that I love you."

Just like that, the door of opportunity will swing open for you as long as you keep knocking. Keep banging on the door. Keep yelling. Picture yourself with a megaphone, speaking louder and louder until people take notice. That's persistence. If you keep trying, keep pushing, keep knocking, it'll happen for you. Your dream can't help but become reality.

Community

You've heard it said time and time again: You are not an island. You are not isolated. You are one person in a community of many. Your community is your family, your neighborhood, your coworkers, your fellow worshippers, your friends and extended family members, even your global community. We are all intertwined, and the actions of one person affect everybody else.

You've also heard, I'm sure, that it takes a village to raise a kid. We have to watch out not only for our own but for all others in our community. I remember that when I was a kid, we had "community checks and balances." My mother wasn't alone in trying to correct me and keep me along the straight and narrow path. Neighbors corrected me as needed. Teachers corrected me. Everybody pulled together to help each young person learn right from wrong and choose the right thing. It was a whole community effort.

> Everyone is aware of the vast difference between a number of men as a chance collection of individuals and the same number as an organized group or community. A community has purpose and plan, and there is in us an almost instinctive recognition of the connection between unity and strength.
>
> *J. Glenn Gray*

A community is a checks and balance organization that helps your immediate family keep you in check. It's people looking out for your home when you're out of town. Checking in on you when you're under the weather. Helping kids with homework. Bringing you food when you need it. To me, that's what the ideal community is, and that's what we need to strive for in our neighborhoods. All of us can ultimately create our destinies and reach our dreams when we work together and help each other along. Living in a community is just that—a "family" of people watching out for each other and helping one another move forward. When any member of that community progresses, the whole community progresses as well. And when every community member moves forward, the whole community benefits immensely.

God

I could not have done a thing in my life without God ever-present, ever-guiding me patiently and without ceasing. God has never given up on me, and I want to show my gratitude and respect by never, ever giving up on God and by serving Him in all of my words, thoughts, actions, and deeds. You have to have hope, you have to have persistence, and you have to be part of a healthy community, but if you don't have God, you have nothing. God is number one. God is.

> God is the total sum of life itself.

God is there for you, even when you don't think He is. God has given you grace and mercy. I know some people who think they're very successful without God. They think they did it all themselves. These folks only *think* they're successful. They're not really living; they're merely existing. You, too, may go through a period of time thinking that you've done it all on your own. But be aware, it's only a matter of time before you realize that you *need* God in your life. I speak from personal experience. I had it all, the so-called "American Dream"—nice house, nice job, and nice cars. On the outside I was successful, but on the inside I felt dead. It was only when I embraced Jesus as my personal savior that a light came on and I had significance in my life. I invite you to pray and receive him as your personal savior. This is how we become successful in God's eyes. Seek God.

What's Next?

Life is a great, big, wonderful adventure, and there's always something that awaits each of us just around the corner. With God as your CEO and hope, persistence, and community as your board members, you are well equipped to embrace the adventure and leave your legacy along the way! What's your legacy going to be? When I'm dead and my spirit has moved on, I want the marker on my grave to read, "Here lies a man who went above and beyond to help people." That's how I want to be remembered. How will you be remembered?

We all want to live comfortably, but I want to stress that money and material things won't make you happy. They may make you comfortable, but happiness comes from within yourself. I enjoyed working at the law firm with my good friend Bryan Boysaw, but I left because it was time for me to focus completely on my mission to empower youth through Urban Youth Development. Bryan was great. He offered to double my salary *every year* if I agreed to stay on. He offered to get me a fully loaded Mercedes Benz. I was touched and truly humbled by his generous offers. But in the end, I knew what I had to do. I knew I had to leave the law firm and focus on building up youth. And my friend understood that I needed to move on.

> As surely as we are driven to live, we are driven to serve spiritual ends that surpass our own interests... We are not only in need of God but also in need of serving His ends, and these ends are in need of us.
>
> *Abraham Joshua Heschel*

You have a mission, a purpose, as well. That's part of the adventure of life: Discovering your own unique God-given mission and following through with it. The way I see it, working for the Lord is the best-paying job you can ever have! Every day I wake up and I thank God that I'm still breathing. I look at my children and my wife and I see the love of God in them, and I am deeply grateful. I'm not afraid of the future, because I know that whatever it holds, God's going to be there with me, guiding me every step of the way. With God by your side, I know that you too will have a wonderful life, and that despite the scars along the way, you'll be a fantastic success. Believe it.

Success Story

Mattie Stepanek, Author & Peacemaker

He dreamed of becoming an "ambassador of humanity," and by all accounts Mattie Joseph Thaddeus Stepanek reached that magnificent goal. He wrote many poems that touch the heart and lift people up. His seven books—one a collaboration with former president Jimmy Carter—made it to the New York Times Bestseller's list. One of his close friends created and released a music album featuring Mattie's poetry; the album reached #15 on the U.S. Top Country Chart. As an inspirational speaker, Mattie addressed the important topics of peace and global tolerance in front of diverse audiences, from schoolchildren to business leaders to church groups across America. He appeared on Oprah, Larry King Live, and The Today Show, among other television programs.

Mattie accomplished all of this by the age of thirteen. He thoroughly enjoyed touring the country and sharing his message of peace, and he made friends wherever he went. Because he was born with a rare form of muscular dystrophy (MD), he wasn't able to reach his goal of becoming a daddy. The disease cut his life short; he passed away in 2004 a few weeks before his fourteenth birthday. But he did achieve his dreams of being an inspirational speaker, an ambassador for peace, and a writer. Each day he lived by his motto, which was, "Think gently, speak gently, live gently." Mattie attributed his strength to God, to his mom, and to all of the people who became a part of his circle of life. He was blessed with friends; nearly 1,350 people attended his funeral, where Jimmy Carter read his eulogy.

This young man who held on to hope every moment of his life and who has inspired millions through his heartfelt poetry teaches us to live every minute to the fullest. Perhaps if we take Mattie's words to heart, we will be inspired to use our gifts and talents to make this a better world. To brighten someone's day. To live with an outlook of joy and gratitude. Here are Mattie's words from his poem, For Our World, which he wrote on September 11, 2001. You can see the entire poem at MattieOnline.com, where it is reprinted with permission from his book *Hope Through Heartsongs*, published by Hyperion:

"We have, we are, a mosaic of gifts
To nurture, to offer, to accept.
We need to be.
Just be.
Be for a moment.
Kind and gentle, innocent and trusting,
Like children and lambs,
Never judging or vengeful
Like the judging and vengeful.
And now, let us pray,
Differently, yet together,

Before there is no earth, no life,
No chance for peace."

© Matthew Joseph Thaddeus Stepanek

e|LIVE

listen|imagine|view|experience

AUDIO BOOK DOWNLOAD INCLUDED WITH THIS BOOK!

In your hands you hold a complete digital entertainment package. Besides purchasing the paper version of this book, this book includes a free download of the audio version of this book. Simply use the code listed below when visiting our website. Once downloaded to your computer, you can listen to the book through our computer's speakers, burn it to an audio CD or save the file to your portable usic device (such as Apple's popular iPod) and listen on the go!

How to get your free audio book digital download:

1. Visit www.tatepublishing.com and click on the e|LIVE logo on the home page.
   Enter the following coupon code:
   ?9-e499-c51b-a7b2-77fa-b9f8-dba6-f98e.
   :nload the audio book from your e|LIVE digital locker and begin ving your new digital entertainment package today!